BELIEVE YOU CAN
LIVE A LIFE YOU LOVE
AT 50+

Compiled & Edited
by

SUE WILLIAMS

Acknowledgements

THIS BOOK TRULY is a team effort. It demonstrates the power of connection, creativity, collaboration and contribution at their best. These important qualities underpin the paradigm shift that is currently taking place in our world and in business.

The intention of the authors is to share the insights gleaned from their own journeys to demonstrate the powerful transformations that occur when we are able to believe. To believe that we are here for a purpose, and that we have all of the inner resources we need to succeed on our own terms as we move into our fifties and beyond. I thank all of the contributors for demonstrating that miracles happen when we realise the power that comes from believing in our own unique gifts and talents.

Sincere thanks go to all those who have contributed, supported and encouraged me in bringing this project to fruition. Thank you for believing in me, as I believe in you!

The deepest gratitude goes to each author and poet who has contributed to this book.

Sue Williams

Praise For This Book

"Imagine if you could have thirty-one personal coaches, all experts in their field of life experience, helping you choose and shape the life you were meant to live?

Sue Williams has brought together thirty-one "every women" to tell their stories of what it can be like for a woman to be over fifty and in control of her choices, her creativity and her contentment. Each contribution shares tips and tools that can help us search inside ourselves, where the real answers lie.

The honest and poignant stories shared in this anthology will inspire you and encourage you to make midlife your best life. They will give new meaning to the old question, "If not now, when?" You will find in them permission—as if you needed permission—to be a "late bloomer", and a powerful, successful one at that.

In these stories we can see how often, when we least expect it, life shifts and new unexpected experiences happen that uplift us so that we can discover the skills and strengths to stretch beyond our wildest imaginings.

I highly recommend *Believe You Can Live a Life You Love at 50+* for any woman asking herself, "Who am I, really?" or "Is this all?" or "Can there possibly be more?"

Thanks so much, Sue, for the opportunity to feel renewed by these empowering stories!"

Carolyn Hamilton. Author, Artist and Success Coach
for Memoir Writers. www.carolynvhamilton.com

"With approaching fifty or "the big 5 0" as it's often named, next year, I felt inspired to read this collection of short stories celebrating living a fulfilled life at this mid-life age.

We frequently hear of the phrase "mid-life crisis" and it's refreshing to instead see how these wonderful folks took this time in their life to truly dig deep within and find purpose through various means. The stories are succinct but they each leave us with a meaningful message and provide a few simple, yet remarkably helpful tips to introduce in our own lives to improve it in some way.

The stories range from how physical health challenges have impacted a person's life, turning low self-esteem on its head, experiences of exciting world travel, finding ways to heal naturally and transforming a poor money mindset. There are many others packed full of wisdom and I trust I have whetted your appetite to explore these for yourself.

Poems from the soul are weaved throughout the pages which beautifully pulls the inspiring stories together into this collaboration of truths.

I believe in the power of a true story as each person has a story to tell that can help another and this book will not leave the reader short of inspiration"

Samantha Houghton, Ghostwriter and book mentor.
www.samanthahoughton.co.uk

"I believe in the power of words, storytelling and sharing unapologetically from the heart.

Sue Williams in *Believe You Can Live a Life You Love at 50+* weaves poetry and real-life stories from women who have found meaning and purpose again. Every single story and poem generously and courageously shared in this book will help you look inside irrespective of the stage and age you may be at. Every single hint and tip is an offering to help you believe in your unique essence, in your soul wisdom and self value. All these women share their *journey to claiming gold* by digging deeper and deeper, armed with faith, compassion and trust, even when challenged by obstacles on the way.

As I approach 50 soon, I've had the honour to connect with the spirit of these warrior women contributors, women who after going over crossroads and life changes urge us to drop the guard, remove the mask and be real.

This book promises the reader the inspiration to see yourself from a different angle, the permission to change the way you see your life and set yourself free from all the "shoulds"; to press pause and connect with the "heart space" - this is where your precious gold lies - waiting to be mined and claimed back.

Time to say YES to your inner muse and your unique voice!

Time to embrace more of your precious gold *with all its perfect imperfections*.

Time to step up, share your light and shine bright!"

— ChriSOULa Sirigou founder of The Golden Muse Institute: School of Colour Therapy Studies, broadcaster and author of the award-winning anthology "The Book of Soulful Musings: Living LIFE with Love Intention, Flow, Ease" www.ChrisoulaSirigou.com

"There is something rather wonderful reading about women 'of a certain age' who in spite of what life throws at them, live their lives with grace and courage - and sheer determination to thrive. I love the gritty honesty of the stories in this book, enhanced by Sue's insightful poems - yes indeed, words do matter.

The more stories we women share, the more women's lives we will impact in a wonderfully supportive way. Bravo to the women who have shared their stories here and to Sue for collecting them all into this enlightening book"

Susie Mackie, photographer,
author and founder of Women of Spirit
www.womenofspirit.co.uk

Foreword

I WAS ASKED BY Sue to read through the stories in this book at a pivotal time for me. Not only was I just weeks away from my 50th birthday, I was also about to take voluntary exit from a 30-year career in the Civil Service. To say this was a tumultuous time for me is rather an understatement.

Now, at 50, I am feeling the pressure of this milestone age and the perceived need to make the most of my future. I remain unsure as to whether my choice to leave a secure job will turn out to be as many people say it will be: - 'the best decision of my life.' Will I develop my businesses further? Will I become an author? Will I combine these with another job, or not? Will I have enough money? Will I cope with not going into an office every day? Will my family cope with me being at home? There are so many things that I am unsure about.

I feel very blessed to have had the opportunity to read about the amazing journeys of the women 50 and over in this book. Many have faced adversity, personal tragedy, illness, huge transitions and made big changes in the way they live their lives.

I have learned how they have developed their self-belief, followed their intuition, tried new things, achieved their goals. They talk of the way life changes for many as we grow older, such as differences in our relationships with partners, experiencing loss, children leaving home and the menopause arriving.

These changes are happening in my life too, along with my changing work status. I feel uncertain and unsettled but am also aware that within me there is a sense of excitement about the opportunity to lead a life that will be different. I feel proud that I am taking a chance, not staying within my comfort zone and am willing to try something new. I know some would call me 'reckless.'

Do I believe in myself enough to know that things will work out? Do I believe that I am enough, that my uniqueness will see me through? In truth the answer is 'no' some days.

For me, this is where a book like this really helps and I suspect Sue knew that it would help me too. I love finding out about others, their journey, the things that have helped shape them, why they do what they do now. Some might call me just plain nosey, but for me it is all about what we can learn from others, how they can inspire us and how we might apply that in our lives. Not in a copy-cat, do as they do kind of way, but in a way that takes from them what feels authentic for us.

I know that as the months go by and I endeavour to just 'BE' for a while, to really find out about myself and discover where the next steps of my life will take me, that I will come back to this book time and time again. It will help me believe that I can do 'this,' whatever the new post 50 'this' is.

I am certainly going to try out many of the tools, techniques and exercises the contributors suggest, including journaling and writing poetry. I have a lifelong love of writing so I will develop this further, perhaps with short stories. I've certainly picked up the message from many of the contributors about the importance of doing what you love. I'm also going to do the mirror exercises, ask myself searching questions, challenge my limiting beliefs and walk in nature. I keep wondering about yoga and meditation too, so maybe now is the time to give those a try, what have I got to lose?

So, thank you to Sue for putting this anthology together as a resource to support women like me, 50 plus and wondering what more there is to life and whether they are good enough, strong enough and brave enough to reach their potential and achieve their dreams. Thank you also to the women who have shared their stories with the aim of helping others. I'm sure many of them have also boosted their own self-belief as they have reflected on what they have overcome and their personal successes.

Susan Brookes-Morris – ex Civil Servant and founder of Positive Publicity and Positive Kids.

CONTENTS

Transform Midlife to MY Life

"Tell me, what is it you plan to do with
your one wild and precious life?"
— Mary Oliver.

KNOW YOU FEEL apprehensive right now reading these words. You feel as if your life is far from wild, so far from it, in fact that you feel world-weary and worn down by the daily routine. More like the dishcloth wrung out by the sink that the sparkly dishes.

When do you even remember feeling remotely sparkly? How long is it since you last went shopping for a shiny new dress, rather than making do with the tried and tested, somewhat frumpy staples languishing in your wardrobe?

I get it. I understand where you are at right now – I know the feeling of wanting to be somewhere else, anywhere else than where you are right now.

The Midlife Malaise

You catch yourself waking up once again with a resigned sigh, blearily looking round at your oh so familiar surroundings, however lovely they may be, unenthusiastically thinking "there must be more to life than this." World-weary and worn down by the daily routine, you experience a niggling sense of dissatisfaction with your life, but don't know why or what to do about it. You feel as if time is slipping by inexorably, and yet find it harder and harder to drag yourself out of bed each day. You catch yourself wondering where that youthful, enthusiastic person you once were has gone. It is as if she has taken a permanent duvet day, and you feel too disenchanted with life to even bother imagining you can make your dreams a reality.

If this sounds like you, be assured - you are certainly not alone. Approaching and entering their fifties is often a time of major change and re-evaluation for women, not least prompted by the onset of the menopause. Along with common physical symptoms such as the dreaded hot flushes, night sweats and restless nights, you may also experience a gnawing sense that something is wrong with your life. Yet you struggle to pinpoint exactly what it is.

Such feelings of confusion are recognised as part of experiencing a midlife crisis. Well-documented, this phenomenon is believed to start around the age of 44 onwards, stretching into the early to late 50s for many. A time when many women, like you, seek guidance and support to help work through their concerns, to re-evaluate their lives; to set and achieve new goals to bring a sense of satisfaction and purpose going forward.

In 2017, Forbes Coaches Council identified various signs that someone has entered a midlife crisis, drawn from thousands of coaching clients. Their experiences include:

- A sense of living life on autopilot
- Feelings of apathy, even a dread of getting out of bed
- Inability to make decisions
- Seeking a bigger purpose in life
- A sense that their existing life feels like it is no longer working
- Feeling unsatisfied despite being successful
- Becoming aware of the clock ticking
- Feeling unclear about what direction to take

If any of these tell-tale signs feels strikingly familiar, and you increasingly feel as though you are sleepwalking through life, don't worry! I have collated the stories, hints and tips in *Believe You Can Live a Life You Love at 50+* to bring solace and support, and to help you to revolutionise your thinking and approach.

A time of change, reflection and re-evaluation

Mary Oliver's question was certainly pertinent to me when, at the age of 51, I chose to retire early from a career in the Civil Service; simultaneously suffering the loss of both my parents within a year of each other. With these constants in my life gone, I suddenly felt uncertain of who I was and how to proceed.

Perhaps, like me, you also face major upheaval? Other common changes around this time include the kids flying the nest, leaving a huge gap in your life. Or, it could be that the career you worked so hard for has lost its allure, and you are tired of feeling stressed and overwhelmed. Or, maybe you are faced with the worry of aging parents or relatives who increasingly need more of your attention and support.

If you can relate to these or other cataclysmic changes in your life, take a moment to reflect. Recall those youthful dreams and challenges you have either achieved or firmly placed on the back burner. Pause to consider how your life has taken unexpected twists and turns, and how you have navigated a few inconvenient potholes and unpleasant bumps in the road. It may even be that the things that once seemed incredibly important to you no longer hold the same urgent pull, now you face the uncertainty of change.

Consider the signals glaring before you, calling you to re-evaluate your circumstances. Are you facing a red light, urgently indicating a need to stop? Pause and ask yourself how often do you do things that you enjoy? Things that light you up, make you come alive? If you are undergoing significant life changes that allow you to take more time for yourself, why not take the opportunity to branch out and try something new. Something invigorating that will bring a renewed sense of joy, purpose or passion into your life?

This is a time when many begin to feel a strong need to ensure their life has meaning, a desire to fulfil their life purpose and make a difference.

So, I ask you again, what do you plan to do with your one wild and precious life?

New beginnings

Part of my own new beginning involved writing poetry; a happy and unexpected outcome experienced when experimenting with a journaling technique called "Morning Pages." This technique is taken from a book called *The Artists Way*, authored by Julia Cameron. It involves writing 3 full pages of hand-written, free-flowing writing first thing each morning. It's a great way to offload any repetitive thoughts, doubts or fears you may find endlessly running around your brain. Sometimes, a simple, everyday solution like a pen, a pad of paper and a commitment to try something new leads to unanticipated consequences.

After expressing my thoughts on the pages of a crisp, new journal for a couple of weeks, my writing surprised me by emerging in rhyme! I later wrote my rallying poem, Believe! the catalyst that eventually led me to instigate and publish the *Believe You Can* series of books; urging me as it did to "stand up, stand up, be bold, be strong". For someone who had felt herself increasingly fading into the background, these words acted as a wakeup call, spurring me forward to develop my long-neglected writing and publishing dreams. I also had the thrill of standing on stage to read Believe! out loud in front of 200 women at an event, and later achieved a gold award for my inspirational Believe oracle cards app and ran events of my own.

What unrealised dreams secretly lie dormant in a hidden corner of your mind; I wonder? How might you coax them to reappear? I and the other authors in this book have all faced a turning point. We want to help you to realise your dreams and desires too!

Transform midlife to MY life

One powerful realisation for me was how I had spent much of my life hiding, fearing what people will think, scared to make mistakes; terrified of not fitting in. As Dr. Seuss said, "why fit in when we were born to stand out?"

Yet how do we stand out if our sense of self is not strong? One of the simplest things we can do is to follow Mary Oliver's example, and do what we love, that has meaning for us. Even taking regular walks in nature can bring solace and a new perspective. Ask yourself, "what brings me joy?"

What is more, I believe that some of us are destined to be late developers. An astrology report I ordered advised that, due to the position of Capricorn in my birth chart, this applied to me. Whether you follow astrology or not doesn't matter. For me, this struck a chord - I chose early retirement to regain control of my life.

As you read these powerful true stories written by women who have dug deep to find the self-belief to face their fears and the confidence to overcome their challenges, let *Believe You Can Live a Life You Love at 50+* provide the stimulus to believe in yourself a little more. Choose to focus on your own needs as you let go of old, false, limiting beliefs. Allow the stories, strategies, hints and tips, tried and tested by each author, to help you find the inner strength to face your fears and achieve the level of happiness, sense of purpose and inner fulfilment you truly deserve.

Compiling and editing this book of inspirational stories to encourage others to 'seize the day' is part of my purpose. I invite you to join us and celebrate the collected, empowering energy of women in their 50s and above!

Sue Williams

BELIEVE!

Stand up, stand up! Be bold, be strong.
Your talent, on world stage, truly does belong!
You are a beacon, shining bright,
Birthed to emerge, grow, and shine your inner light.

It is a crime to leave talent, dusty on a rickety, hidden shelf,
Set out your stall; allow true expression
of your amazing inner self.
Surely, you will experience some discomfort as you stretch,
far better than staying a self-defeating, self-pitying little wretch?
Rather, as you experience movement,
create life-changing shifts,
you will, newly emboldened, dare to share your gifts!

Life is truly meant for us to live; by our own example, given
To those, like us, who have sometimes been
Squashed, ignored, or diligently working;
self-effacing, behind a screen
Of uniformity; water poured on burning fire,
Quashed down, made damp squib of all passion and desire.

And, as others bask in your new golden glow,
It helps for them, also to know,
That they have their own miracles to perform,
Whether on a stage, or as more often is the norm,
In their own families and communities,
through their daily life and deeds.

Do great work; sow and nurture the seeds
Of positivity, purposefulness and joy,
With which we all entered this world to buoy

Up ourselves and others,
manifest the birth right of our mothers,
As we mix with friends, many others,
who enter into our life's stratosphere.
All add dark and shade, maybe cause us to shed a tear,
Perhaps of joy or sometimes pain,
so, ultimately, of our own truth, understanding we gain.

Right here and now, we need to show,
Through heartfelt determination,
strength of courage,
We all have the power to foster our own abilities, to grow;
Achieve our birth right to succeed; root out the dreaded weed
That with stranglehold choked down
our well-intentioned schemes,
Left us struggling with dashed hopes, and broken,
once beautiful dreams.

So, meaning-full, join us to create,
an interwoven, brilliant picture to which all can relate!
As one voice, stand up and state:

"We are here to live mindfully in this life,
we choose creativity, positive intent over unrewarding strife
and as we choose to change how we ourselves perceive,
in our own dreams, our legacy, our power, we truly believe!"

~ Sue Williams ~

From Social Anxiety to Self-esteem and Success

Bernadette Sarginson

'How does one become a Butterfly?' she asked pensively.
'You must want to fly so much you are willing
to give up being a Caterpillar'.
— Dr Wayne Dyer

I HAD A VERY happy childhood, generally speaking. I was born in 1968, and spent my early years growing up in the 1970's with all the freedom and fun that was available in the years before 'health & safety' intervened. Many a fabulous day was spent in the holidays out climbing, exploring or bike riding with my friends, staying out for hours on end without a care in the world.

I remember I always loved going to school. First to the Infants (as it was called in those days) and then to Junior School. I just loved learning, and being in the classroom surrounded by my friends. Such was my joy for living that I found delight in even the most mundane and repetitive of tasks. One specific example I recall is that I'd always colour-coordinate the washing when I hung it out on the line for mum, going from black through every colour of the rainbow to the lightest coloured garment in a sophisticated flow and deliberate blending of the colours.

I grew up on a housing estate and money was often tight. Keen gardeners, my parents always used most of our modest sized back garden to grow their own vegetables (much healthier and cheaper than buying from the shops). One of my most treasured memories is of being in school when the teacher read out a list of produce, and asked the class by show of hands whether we grew each individual variety at home. I remember feeling so proud that I was the only person that raised my hand for every single item mentioned.

My love of nature and connection with the outdoors has stayed with me throughout my lifetime and, I'm delighted to say, the 'green-fingered' gene has been lovingly passed on to me when it comes to gardening.

I was a bright child and, if I'm honest, I always felt a little different from my friends about the way I looked at the world, the way I would think so deeply about things, and the way I processed and allowed all my experiences to shape who I am today. You could almost say that I have always felt pulled towards a higher purpose.

What I didn't know during my early years was that I had a bladder condition which meant that I rarely felt the sensation of needing the toilet during the night, so I wet the bed far longer than expected. As an adult, I was able to have the simple diagnosis and treatment to fix this condition, but as a child growing up when parenting was completely different to how it is today, I found the whole experience devastating. I struggled with feelings of shame through desperately wanting to wake up dry. It wasn't necessarily what my parents said or did in response to my bed-wetting but it was all about how I internalised what was happening.

It did eventually stop when I was about ten years old but the whole experience had already left its' mark by this point and would shape the way I felt about myself for many years to come.

During my teenage years and early twenties, I developed social anxiety and would experience crushing discomfort with cheeks burning bright any time I felt like the spotlight was on me. It didn't happen all the time and in certain situations I was ok, so most of my close family and friends were not even aware of what was going on in other areas of my life. This continued well into my twenties and through university, and became the catalyst for sparking a life-long interest in self-awareness and personal development.

I qualified as a solicitor in 1993 and practised successfully for several years, but I always felt that something was missing. I wanted to express more of my creativity, so I left the law after getting married and started my first business. It wasn't hugely successful on one level, yet on another level it was massively successful, teaching me many lessons of business in the real world that you just can't learn from a text book. Fast forward a few more years and I moved back into law, via the circuitous route of corporate tax at one of the big accounting firms.

My first beautiful daughter arrived in the world when I was 35 years old, and when baby number two was due to arrive two years later, I knew that I needed to move out of law permanently. I was becoming less and less satisfied with my work, and the practicalities of juggling a very young family with a full-time legal career were becoming increasingly difficult. Heavily pregnant and within days of giving birth, I stumbled upon an advertisement in a magazine for a weight loss franchise that was recruiting, and it grabbed my attention. The ethos of the company, the overwhelming emphasis on the mind-set and personal development of the clients I'd be working with and the therapeutic environment I'd be creating were all huge draws for me. I sent off for the information and, after much deliberation, decided to take the leap of faith and enroll for what would become a permanent career change into the field of personal empowerment.

Over the next six years, my focus was on people, passion and purpose and I loved every minute of watching my clients transform into butterflies and find their wings. It was a steep learning curve at the start, but I knew deep down that I had found my true path, supporting my clients within the structure of the programme I was delivering, whilst bringing in my own unique insights, perspectives and wisdom with a deep sense of empathy, care and compassion.

This move in 2005 was the first time in my life I had ever fully appreciated how powerful our thoughts are; how they drive and shape everything; and how you *always* have a choice whether to engage with or believe your thoughts. I came to realise that within my legal background I had, until this point, been blinkered about self-awareness. This new learning opened up a whole new world of connection and understanding for me.

Since then I have committed my life to working in personal empowerment with people in all sorts of circumstances and I remain committed to this day. The journey hasn't always been easy and, as a small business, it's fair to say that the years have had their ups and downs. A few years ago, parts of my old 'shadow-self' from those early years started to reappear. Scary at first, but it proved to be the best gift I could have wished for, giving me with great insight into my own thoughts and feelings.

In February 2016 I was invited to South Africa for some training for entrepreneurs. The trip was life-changing in so many ways. The land in South Africa is very spiritual and energetically charged and I had instinct after instinct about how to move my business forward. It was from there that I got real clarity and belief in my life purpose and it's also where I developed my own success system around self-esteem. It's a simple, effective, repeatable and sustainable system to reduce anxiety and re-balance self-esteem and a sense of self-worth – any time, *every time,* and it's for women and men with high success on the outside yet low spirit on the inside.

Later that year, things became challenging with business. As we approached the winter months, I started to nose-dive into a very difficult place mentally and emotionally, completely losing my way spiritually. On the outside everything seemed fine most of the time, but on the inside, I was really struggling with how I felt about myself, and with several other aspects of my life.

But this time something was different.

During this really tough period, instead of completely collapsing into it, I was able to observe the experience from the side-lines whilst feeling the full weight of it. Each time I sank a little further I kept asking myself, 'what do I need to help me find a way through this?'

Each time I asked, my intuition dutifully responded.

This happened often during those months and with each new insight, my new system was enhanced. I used my own pain and suffering positively, coupled with my passionate desire to empower other people to be able to move forward without needing anyone or anything else whenever they hit a low point.

I came through the whole experience not just with new learning, but with a renewed self-belief, and a deep sense that all my prior learnings and experiences had become fully embedded and integrated into my life and purpose, ready for the next chapter.

I spent 2017 writing my programme and laying the groundwork for my first book so that in February 2018 as I turned 50, my programme and business launched on-line. My first book 'Climb Your S.T.A.I.R.™ of Self-Confidence' was published later that same year.

Finally, at age 50, I was able to become properly visible and show the world who I am and what I stand for. I am passionate about people and passionate about self-empowerment. I have eventually reached a point where I can fully accept myself for who I am and what I can bring. I now embrace my own experiences, perspective and wisdom as completely valid and valuable. I am free of self-doubt because I have reconnected with spirit in such a profound way that I have an inner knowing that everything will work out exactly as it is meant to. But I don't just sit back and wait for things to happen. It's only through having your eyes wide open to opportunities that you will see them when they arise, so I always trust my instinct if it tells me to move forward.

My focus now is on living a healthy life of service and purpose, more so than I have ever done before. And I walk the talk of my own system for self-esteem, always navigating and course-correcting my thoughts, mind-set and responses both internal and external.

What I do now is a world away from where I started my career as a solicitor. Back then it was all about rules, regulations and litigation. Now, my world is based on trust, experience, wisdom, instinct and inner knowing. And this is something that is only possible because I have lived through half a century and have the privilege of having a whole wealth of life experience behind me. I now see every single experience I have had in my life as a gift that was divinely delivered to allow me to become the person I am today.

My three key recommended habits are;

1. Always remember you have a choice with how to think, feel and behave. Your thoughts drive your feelings and behaviour and you can *always* choose not to engage with any unhelpful, negative thoughts and take the energy away from them.

2. Live mindfully and in the moment, with gratitude, at all times. It's so easy to get tied up in replaying situations, conversations and decisions from the past or focusing excessively on the future and worrying about things that may never happen. Being present in the moment takes patience, practise and focus but the rewards of doing so are exponential.

3. Always pause before responding to any situation and never act from a knee-jerk response unless it is positive and supports you. Lead with compassion, and train yourself to see every challenging situation from at least one other perspective, always seeking out the positive intention behind what the other person is saying or doing.

Bernadette Sarginson is a former lawyer turned empowerment coach and mentor; an Intuitive with a mission. Working in a bespoke and unique way, she brings a powerful mixture of life experience, intuitive wisdom, education and coaching to her work to enable you to raise your game both personally and professionally.

She has coached and mentored hundreds of individuals and groups through long term change management and personal development.

From over-coming her own self-doubt, she created the Spirit Level Success™ System – Six Secrets of Self-Esteem which is guaranteed to reduce anxiety, and re-balance your self-esteem and sense of self-worth any time, every time.

Visit www.spiritlevelsuccess.com to download your free copy of 'You Are Enough'.

UNLEASHED

Here stands a woman, strong, proud and brave,
Statuesque in beauty, gentle with grace;
Owns the attention, from others once craved.
Caring concern etched on her face

For all humanity's lost hopes and dreams;
Swept away on the winds of a long-forgotten time,
Buried in a morass of degradation, renegade schemes,
Her true essence recovered through ballerina rhyme.

Unleash the secret of who you really are.
Who stole your sparkle, left but a scar?
Leave them behind you, cut negative ties,
No space in this life for treachery and lies.

Joyfully reclaim your soft, creative soul,
Own your perfection; authentic, whole.

Sue Williams

Survival by Natural Healing

Bernadette Whiteside

Someone once told me:
"Don't think of it as cancer think of it as damaged cells."

THIS WAS PROBABLY the best advice I had heard and the most important recommendation I can pass on to anyone who is suffering from the same damaged cells as me.

My journey started in February 2015, three months after my 50th birthday. I had just returned from the most wonderful five-month solo tour of Asia and Australia. I was on a natural high and feeling very good about life. In fact, I started to study again so I could return to Asia and teach English. Three months later I got my TEFL results. I passed. I was delighted and started to look for jobs in Cambodia.

Little did I know that my dream to work abroad would be halted indefinitely and life had a totally different plan for me.

I've heard it said that we choose our life before we are born. We choose our parents to match the lessons we must learn in this incarnation and we select our blueprint for our journey through life, mapping out the whole course, all before we are born.

So, knowing this I have to ask the question why did I choose such a difficult life? What can I learn from struggling through the years, from a painful marriage and equally hurtful divorce, and mostly what is there that I have to learn from four years of battling cancer and trying to outlive this curse that just keeps on returning?

There must be a big lesson there somewhere. I must be so dense that it's taken me four years to discover it. And who says I have? I suppose I haven't if I'm still walking around carrying these lumps around with me. Five painful, stubborn tumours that are so deep inside the chest wall they are almost in my back. Damn tumours which hurt so much I need to medicate every four hours or I'll know about it. Infected lymph nodes, missing lymph nodes, itchy skin, painful scars, lumpectomy, mastectomy, reconstruction surgery, pic lines, blood clot, breathlessness, chemo brain, cancer fatigue, fear in all capacities. These are just a few words in my new vocabulary.

My first diagnosis was left breast cancer. Triple negative cancer. One of the worse kinds. If you hear these words be prepared to fight. I collapsed to my knees when I heard my diagnosis. To comfort mum and I the nurse said all the cancer would be removed in the lumpectomy. I couldn't even hear her. I had to take leaflets home to explain everything to me because everything was a blur.

I had the surgery and I recovered. I started eight rounds of chemo. My hair fell out after the first cycle. Tiny strands at first then huge clumps of it fell onto the bathroom floor until my feet were covered in masses of blonde thick waves that took me years to grow. I screamed at the sight. It was grotesque, scary in its surreal state. I stared at myself in the mirror but did not recognise the person staring back at me. I searched the deformed frame for some sign of resemblance then I searched again and still I found none.

That evening a barber shaved the remaining tufts from my skull and I took to wearing scarves. I must say I really enjoyed wearing them. They were easy to wear, quick and comfortable and one of mine reminded me of a 1940's farm girl so I became playful with them, changing colours and styles, sometimes even going outdoors without anything on my head at all. But that was only on hot days.

The effects of chemo didn't hit me until day five. After it was administered, I turned into a lifeless breathing corpse. I think cancer fatigue can only be truly appreciated by other cancer sufferers. It is a tiredness that totally disables you. It had me flat on my back for two weeks out of every four. I didn't even have the energy to speak. By the time I felt back to normal, it was time for chemo again.

Three months into chemo I experienced severe stomach pain and had to be rushed back to the hospital. After blood tests and a colonoscopy, the doctor came to see me with this news. "Bernadette I'm sorry to inform you, you have colon cancer. You need an operation immediately."

We were floored, my mum, my sister and me. A sudden quiet eeriness filled the room. I think it was fear and disbelief. The doctor continued to explain the procedure, but I didn't hear any of it. I sat staring out of the window and understood why none of them opened, because if they did people like me would jump through them.

The next morning, I had my operation, the pain of recovery was unimaginable. So unbearable in its intensity, that looking back I don't know how I survived.

Chemo was interrupted for two months while I recovered. Whoopie. Party time.

I wish I could say I did party a lot but the truth was I was in agony, I was tender, I was in bed a lot and suffering from depression.

Whilst everybody around me got on with living I felt like I was sewn into the bed sheets unable to escape. People were going on holiday, getting married, having parties and all I could do was lay down. I was crumbling under the weight of deep sadness.

In my despair I started to listen to meditative music. I found it so comforting that even today, four years later I need it to fall asleep. Powerful Healing Theta Meditation 528hz on YouTube, this was and is my all-time favourite healing music. Another lovely piece of relaxing music is Reiki music. It reminds me of angels, heavenly choral music. So beautiful to listen to when you need peace and hope.

It has become a part of my daily routine. I just love it. Sometimes I walk around the house cleaning to this music, it's so peaceful and uplifting.

Through St Luke's Oncology Department, I started seeing a counsellor to help with my worsening depression. I also had art therapy where I could draw or paint anything I wanted freestyle which I loved because it brought out the child in me. I was never good at art at school but there was no competition here and I relaxed into my classes with a child's enthusiasm and abandonment. I experimented with colours and just drew. I let the crayons or paint brushes flow freely and I followed their direction. It was so beautiful to rewind my mind back to an age of preschool where everything was innocence and carefree. There was no conformity, no rivalry, just an hour of peacefulness, diminished responsibility and sheer joy. It was one of the best healing therapies I did throughout my years at the hospital.

The longest and most rewarding therapy for me was an hour a week with Fiona my counsellor. I spent a year engrossed in my own history exploring side effects of everything that led me to the place I found myself in today. I absolutely loved my time with Fiona. No stone was left unturned, we laughed, I cried, we joked and I delved deeper and deeper until I hit the deepest depth of my whole being. I found it revolutionary.

Six months later I became aware at just how valuable Fiona was to me when an obstruction occurred in my bowel and I was admitted into hospital again for a third operation. It's easy to get lost in this myriad of dates, but this is still 2015 and within eleven months I had 2 cancers, 3 operations, 8 cycles of chemo, 8 infections, one blood transfusion, one blood clot and six months of self-administered daily injections. Now I had hit rock bottom. I was more depressed than ever before and in a great deal of pain.

Never had I once asked Why Me? I was the kind of person who asked Why not me? But sitting in that hospital bed one day listening to my meditative music, I asked God why he gave me so much to deal with. I never heard his answer and I must have missed a message. I laid there as if I was already laying in my coffin and stared blankly out of the window for ten days before I went home on Christmas Eve and began Radiotherapy in January. Five days a week for five weeks. I found it all very exhausting.

I never lost faith in God, I still prayed, I just didn't know if he could hear me. I went inside myself for a long while, often too tired to speak I just fell silent and slept with my inner thoughts.

2016 was a year of recovery for me. My body had been through an awful lot and it was telling me it was shattered and needed to rest. I obliged willingly. I had no strength to argue so I slept and rested whenever I needed to.

Even though my limbs ached and chemo brain plagued me I felt the pull of spring air and in mid-March started to venture more outside. At first, I began to take short walks holding onto mum's arm. The freshness of new air and warm sun breathed energy into my body and I longed for more.

As my body regained its strength in the months that followed, I was more able to take longer walks in the woods and forests nearby. I had days out at the beach and went to National Trust Properties with my new dog which I found at a rescue shelter. I called my new pal Beau. Beau is a beautiful big Chocolate Labrador. I think we rescued each other. We started to go everywhere together, suddenly I was walking for two hours a day. I was so happy to be getting fit again. I started to feel healthier than I had in eighteen months. Life was looking up again.

The summer came and went and I returned to work as a carer for the elderly. I loved my work and took Beau with me. Everybody loved him. He was a good calming energy and brought love and cuddles to all my elderly clients.

At the end of the year my daughter went to work in Tenerife. That was a good sign that things were back to normal.

I continued through to the next year with my healing therapies, enjoying reflexology, counselling, reiki, spirituality and gardening club.

Just as I began to relax into 2017 life changed yet again. Perhaps I was getting too comfortable but whatever the reason the universe stepped in and shook me up.

January 17th my appointment for a scan and a mammogram showed another lump so my surgeon suggested an immediate biopsy.

I got the results at the end of January. Yes, you've guessed it. The cancer just can't leave me alone. It was back.

In March I had a mastectomy with a temporary implant. Everything was fine thankfully.

I was back in hospital in November to replace the implant with a permanent one. All went well and I returned to work a week later.

The year ended well with me celebrating Christmas with a new love. It was happy times. I was grateful for my life, I was still here, feet firmly planted on terracotta ground. My new mantra was don't sweat the small stuff and I didn't.

I felt a new appreciation for everything I had and for everyone special in my life. I no longer took anything for granted.

The deep change in me didn't really surface until August 2018 when for the fourth time I was diagnosed yet again with breast cancer.

What on earth was going on? What was I doing wrong? There must be something I'm doing wrong, what is it?

This time the prognosis was not good. Not even remotely. My doctor confirmed after the usual tests that I had terminal breast cancer. This time there was no cure, no operation, time was running out for me.

I had five tumours deep in the chest wall. There was no coming back from this they said. Take the chemo and extend your life from two to five years otherwise you will be dead in six to nine months. What a choice.

I was so angry. I felt as if I was permanently in the fight or flight mode. I did hours upon hours of research. I was short tempered and fiery. I shouted and screamed a lot and lost myself in a world of grief.

When the doctor hit me with the bad news I fought back and told him he was wrong, that he wasn't God and couldn't determine the estimated time of my death.

I knew instinctively that I didn't want another round of chemo because of the hell it put me through last time but my family were devastated by my admission.

So, under pressure from doctors and family I gave in and surrendered my life unto them. I had two weeks of chemo swiftly followed by six weeks of chest infection, red inflamed feet and hands, mouth ulcers and cancer fatigue so severe I couldn't leave the house for six weeks.

And that's what did it. That was the straw that broke the camel's back. I got mad with myself for not listening to my body and for putting others first. A new rage grew inside of me. I was determined to win on my own terms. I'm not ready to lose this battle at only 54 years old. I'm a survivor, a warrior, I fight on and on. I told the doctor there would be no more chemo for me and he discharged me, telling me to call MacMillan because I was now under palliative care.

Next, I changed my diet. I turned to Vegan food overnight. The first two weeks were horrible. I had many headaches and I was very angry. I didn't want to give up my favourite foods but I felt forced to. I had to learn how to shop and cook but mostly I had to acquire new taste buds.

After hundreds of hours spent researching cancer cures, I narrowed down the therapies that I thought would best work for my type of cancer.

I saw a Kinesiologist to muscle test me against different foods and vitamins.

I started a six-week detox diet that consisted mostly of fruit and raw veg.

I brought bitter apricot kernels because they have cyanide and cyanide eats cancer. I made fruit smoothies for breakfast which contained bee pollen, ginger, apricot kernels, coconut milk, organic honey, spirulina, maca powder, flax seeds, goji berries and exotic fruits that contained cancer healing properties.

I began to take control of my life. I listened to countless testimonials from people who claimed to heal their own cancer and noted their remedies. I read books about how to heal cancer and I brought several vitamins, probiotics, herbs and pastes. I warmed castor oil on a flannel and put it on my tumours, I brought a water filter, gave up tea and alcohol, took Epsom salts in my bath for the magnesium and started to use pure essential oils such as Frankincense, Myrrh, Copaiba and coconut oil. I used a drop under the tongue three times a day and I rubbed the oils on my tumours.

I tried Emotional Freedom Technique therapy which worked wonders for releasing anger and hurt caused by a failed marriage. I have weekly reiki sessions which always give me messages of hope and encouragement. I have tried shamanic healing and spiritual healing to release emotional blockages and cut chords to anything which does not serve me anymore. I had hypnotherapy and every day I use a hyperbaric oxygen chamber.

I pray to God and angels and ask for strength; I listen to Louise Hay and Esther Hicks for positive affirmations and guidance and it all helps.

Everything I do, I do to live. The biggest change in me has been to believe in myself and to love myself unconditionally. Armed with this new power I can see the future as healthy, happy and long.

I think about what I want in my future, I feel it, then I believe it to be so, because with the old me dying there is a new me rebirthing.

I once read that we must all die before we can truly live. I think that is what is happening to me now. My old way of thinking and behaving is dead, I have a new knowledge which arms me with a power and freedom to know I can do this. I can win this battle for life. I'll never stop fighting.

Perhaps I needed a death sentence before I could truly change my life from within by believing in myself and not allowing myself to be dominated by others.

I think I have learnt my lesson.

My tips for anyone on a self-healing journey would be:

1. Always trust your instincts, don't allow yourself to be swayed by anyone who has a different opinion to you. Your opinion is just as valuable.

2. Meditate to receive guided messages. Ask what it is you need to know and wait for the answer to appear.

3. Believe the good truths people tell you about yourself. No self-defamation. This is the creation of self-love.

Bernadette Whiteside is 54 years old and lives with her 24-year-old daughter in Surrey, England. Having worked in accounting and caring for many years she is now retired and concentrating on her creative writing.

Bernadette feels she is on the cusp of discovering herself as a writer. It's been a dream of hers to publish her own book since she won a writing competition at school as a young girl.

As well as contributing to this book, Bernadette has also had a poem published. She is currently working on a children's adventure book for age eight plus.

WHO AM I?

I am the space that breathes life into your words,
I am the song, gloriously chirruped by birds,
I am the trees that stand tall and so proud,
I am the me that I trumpet out loud.
I am the music that lifts up the tune,
I am the light of the sun and the moon.

Sue Williams

You Can Do It

Carole Donnelly

"Whatever the mind can conceive & believe,
the mind can achieve" Napoleon Hill
— Think & Grow Rich

'VE ALWAYS LOVED that quote as it is taken from one of the first books I was recommended to read if I wanted to really change my life and run a successful business.

I'd been working in the social/council housing sector for over 20 years, my children had both left home along with my partner of 7 years and my niece had died - all just before my 50th birthday. Welcome to the worst year of my life, the year that changed everything.

They say life begins at 40, well I can reassure you; life begins when you choose to step up and step into your own life. Hence why the Napoleon Hill quote resonates so much with me. I knew I needed to make a number of changes and this was the year/decade where I would take the control back and really start to enjoy life and step up into my entrepreneurial journey.

My journey into entrepreneurship wasn't conventional and still isn't; not what one would consider as normal, but then again what is normal these days? It really started at an event for women in Birmingham when I was just approaching my 52nd birthday. I'd changed my mind so many times before finally entering the venue. Scared of the unknown, feeling completely out of my depth, enveloped in a world of fear; especially when I entered the room to be greeted by nearly 100 women dressed to impress. I was wearing jeans and a baggy top, normal wear for someone that worked in social housing who wanted to hide and blend in.

My mind went into overdrive: "just who did I think I was being in a room with these aspirational and entrepreneurial ladies?" I felt like a complete fraud and it took all of my courage to remain, especially after getting through the singing and dancing – yes; they really did start the event that way! The simple fact that I was sitting in the second row - bad mistake if you want to escape - ensured I stayed at least until the first break, plus I had paid £100 for the privilege of sitting outside my comfort zone.

Then I started to really listen to the speakers as they shared their stories; their passion, and something just clicked within me; the Napoleon Hill phrase kept popping up, "dream it, believe it and take action" was the message of the day. Yes, I had dreamed it before and yes, I did believe it; but did I really take the action? Now that was the real question that resonated deep within me.

I could do what they were doing. I was a well-educated professional woman; I'd helped to set up a small tenant-led housing company and had single-handily managed it for the last 2 years. I was a budding entrepreneur, but my social mission stopped me from really embracing the 'millionaire mindset.' They kept talking about 6-7 figure businesses, making loads of money. Well, I bet you can imagine the vision I had in my head of a 1980's sitcom YUPPY, can't you?

However, I left the venue on a high after 8 hours of pure inspiration and as I drove home, I began to hatch a plan. I posted on Facebook as soon as I got home, "anyone as daft as me and want to save a bakery?" Within an hour I was chatting to a local lady about a community business idea and how it could work to save an Edwardian bakery from demolition. One week earlier I'd seen the planning application to demolish this old bakery and replace it by building 10 bedsits on the small site.

I live in a conservation area and have campaigned to save a few of our old Victorian buildings from demolition previously; but this was a whole new idea, a whole new way to deliver change and save historic buildings.

Over the next six months I put to together a board of directors, wrote a business plan, launched a community share offer that raised £23,000 in 6 weeks, appeared on the local radio, in the local papers and even on the local BBC and ITV news programmes. I was on a roll, I was going to change the world one bakery, one local community business at a time!

The reality, however, proved different. It wasn't enough to buy the building, and by the summer of 2013 I realised that it wasn't to be. One of the hardest lessons to learn is to let something go. All the old feelings of "who do you think you are?" and not being good enough cropped up for me. Fear took over alongside self-pity; but, if I'm really honest the business model wasn't strong enough and I didn't have the right people with me.

But by then I'd been bitten by the entrepreneurial bug, plus I'd been offered a place at the School for Social Entrepreneurs Start-up Business Programme and, as the bakery wasn't going ahead, I had to come up with another social business quickly or lose my place and the funding that came with it.

I revisited my favourite saying; if I could conceive it, believe it, I could achieve it. My new business was born from my passion for self-development and making a difference in the local community. The Community Empowerment Academy evolved to use all my experience to advise people how to run a community business and take over community assets. (Buildings owned by the Government or Councils that are no longer in use or due to close).

It wasn't easy setting up a community business. The concept was new, no-one really knew what a social enterprise was, so, instead of looking for business opportunities, I went searching for grant funding. I tried to do it all alone and, after a year without making any money, I returned to employment as a Community Development Manager for the local council. Another lesson learnt!

I felt down - I remember writing a short story at 4am which I've shared with every social entrepreneur I know. Yes; I was skint with mounting debts; I was down to my last £30 unable to pay my bills, but I wasn't out. Every lesson we learn takes us closer to our goals. Resilience is what enables us to keep going; sheer bloody mindedness linked with passion, and a need to make a difference also helps.

Running my own business was still at the heart of what I wanted to do; running a social enterprise business. This is the same as a traditional business, it's just what we do with the profits that defines us, alongside the social impact we make in the community or to people's lives. Reinvesting back into the local community "doing business by doing good" is how I like to describe it.

A year or so later another opportunity came up. In February 2016 Coventry City Council announced they were to close the Priory Visitor Centre due to austerity cuts. My campaigning spirit kicked back in and I got involved with the local paper campaign to "Save the Priory." Again, a community business opportunity emerged.

The Priory Visitor Centre and Undercroft contains some of Coventry's original Cathedral, St Mary's and the Benedictine Monastery founded by Lady Godiva and the Earl of Mercia, Leofric in the 11th Century. It was destroyed by King Henry VIII in the 16th Century during the dissolution of the monasteries. St Mary's was the only Cathedral to be destroyed during this period and following a Channel 4 Time Team heritage dig in 1999-2001 some amazing artefacts were unearthed and a Visitor Centre was built in 2003 to display them.

I went to see the local councillor in charge and told her I had a "Cunning Plan" as Baldrick would say; to take over the running of the buildings. Remember my phrase "whatever the mind can conceive and believe."

I had been looking for a new business opportunity and really wanted to demonstrate that a social enterprise business model could work. May 2016 saw me pull together another business plan, get one of the previous bakery directors involved again and an "Expression of Interest" was submitted – a bid to take over the building. By October we had won the right to reopen the building!

It took another 6 months to negotiate the formal lease, but I'd already been given the keys on a number of occasions to host events including a National Heritage Weekend in September and the Global Entrepreneurship Festival in November.

Coventry Priory CIC was formally launched in March 2017 and I reopened the Priory Visitor Centre on the 25th May 2017. I'd been given a £10,000 start-up grant/loan and managed to get another £15,000 of grant funding from 2 other funders.

During 2017 and 2018 I worked on a voluntary basis as a Director, cleaner, tour guide, manager and anything else to keep this amazing venue open to visitors and the local community. I grew the business from a heritage museum into a community event space, which included a community café, art displays, gift shop and a wide variety of events themed around health and wellbeing to tackle social isolation.

There were many times when I felt like walking away and giving up. It cost me a personal relationship as I invested all my time and passion into running this community museum alongside a full-time job. I was fortunate that my day job at Coventry University Social Enterprise enabled me to inspire the next generation of entrepreneurs.

I thought I'd learnt my lessons from the bakery - don't give up the day job until you have got the funds in place to support yourself first. But history has a habit of repeating itself and April 2019 saw me walk away from the university.

April 2019 wasn't a good month as the Priory failed to win a public vote that would have brought in a £47,000 grant and open up an opportunity for £50,000 of 'social' investment at a great interest rate. That would have secured the Priory's future as Coventry headed towards UK City of Culture in 2021. I made the heart wrenching decision to formally close the Priory and returned the keys back to the City Council on the 31st May 2019.

I had been certain 2019 was going to be our and my best year yet as I continued to believe, conceive and achieve. I teamed up with 2 other local entrepreneurs who shared my passion and brought other skills into the business. However, it wasn't meant to be third time lucky for my community business. There was a big fear of taking on debt finance. Without the grant funding it would never have worked; I struggled to get a city on board and ultimately, I chose my health and wellbeing as my priority.

If you dare to dream and follow your dreams, take persistent and consistent action; you really can achieve. It isn't easy, it takes time, it takes real commitment and it can be a very lonely place, but it is so worth it when you reflect and see the real difference you've made.

Would I change anything, Yes, I would, but I still wouldn't have missed the experience and the wealth of knowledge I've built up during the last 10 years and this will enable me to help so many more entrepreneurs as I begin a new journey.

My top three tips for setting up a business are as follows:

1. Be realistic, take your time and plan; there is plenty of advice out there. Grab everything you can and don't be afraid to ask for help. Speak to your local Growth Hub at the Chamber of Commerce and see what's available.

2. Find a mentor who can help you grow and develop your business idea. Listen to their advice and be prepared to research and read. Model yourself on business leaders you admire - read more or alternatively contact me.

3. If it's not working change it; never be afraid to fail as every lesson learnt is valuable. Knowing when to quit takes as much guts as starting a business.

Carole Donnelly is an award winning Social and Traditional Entrepreneur with a passion for making a real difference in her local community and across the UK. Nominated and recognised as a WISE 100 Woman for her contribution to Social Enterprise and helping others establish their own social/community business. Former Director of Coventry Priory CIC (Heritage, Arts and Community Café) Carole now runs her own consultancy inspiring others to scale their business ideas. Contact Carole at caroledonnelly@btinternet.com CJD Consultancy.

AWAKEN

Woman, oh woman, know what you did;
Your light under a bushel, of duty, you hid.
Break free from constraint, cast off those chains,
Shake off the shackles, re-engage your brain.

Women, rise again, filled with fresh hope.
Untie the knot, gently, uncoil the rope.
No longer constrict that elegant throat.
Undo those handcuffs, that make the blood boil,
Rise up from the ashes of oppression and toil.

Dance, Aphrodite, in streams of golden sunlight;
Not designed to whimper, quiver and cower.
Glory in your purpose, brilliant and bright,
Grounded, centred; claim inner power.
Devour the fire, strength reignite.

Unleash the Empress, true Goddess within,
Reject misplaced shame, guilt of original sin.
Bite into juicy apple, sit content in the bower,
A bud, a teardrop, dew on a flower,
Removed from oppression of judgemental glower.

Bloom, glorious Goddess of wisdom, truth and love,
Shower true essence, bathed in white light from above.
Relish the challenge, intent to be, have and do,
Rise one and all, claim true beauty in you.

Sue Williams

It's Never too Late
to Change Your Mind

Caroline Tyrwhitt

"If you think you can or think you can't, you're right".
— Henry Ford

A s a young woman, I would have described myself as confident and in-your-face. I didn't care what people thought. In fact, I loved to court controversy, and I always believed that I could.

I was the girl who at an all girls' grammar school challenged the fact we weren't allowed to wear trousers and got them put on the uniform list.

I did the same in my first job in the banking industry. I recall being challenged by the head of Human Resources for wearing a trouser suit. When he told me women couldn't wear them because some women don't look good in trousers, I looked him up and down and retorted: "some men don't either, but I don't see them being told to wear skirts." Surprisingly, I wasn't fired.

While working at a broking company, a drunken male colleague grabbed my breast on his return from lunch. Unfortunately, my auto response was a right hook, so I was hauled into the director's office and told, "it goes with the job." When I smiled and said that I looked forward to fondling his bits as part of my job, I was quickly hustled out of the office.

At 25, I panicked that life was passing me by and moved to Canada. There I found work in corporate communications, putting myself forward for, and creating exciting jobs, while getting myself qualified for the work I was doing. I loved living in a world that provided equal opportunities and I flourished.

When at 30 I couldn't get a certain job I wanted without a degree, I applied to university. I didn't have the necessary qualifications so went about getting references and testimonials to get in.

I was one of 3,000 vying for 300 places in a top education degree program. At my critical interview I was my cheeky self again. When asked how I was going to entertain my students, I laughed and said I was there to be an educator not a one-man band with cymbals, drums and accordion. Yet I got in.

So how did I find myself fat, 50, in the doldrums and feeling like I had failed? Read on…

When I graduated university with not one but two degrees, I returned to England. I remember being so excited to bring my knowledge and experience of teaching disenfranchised inner-city children to England, to help them break through barriers and achieve, ready to take on and change the world.

I was so shocked that no-one cared what I knew, what I had learned.

Because I wasn't trained in England, I wasn't considered a properly qualified teacher. They paid teachers from abroad peanuts, gave us little support and told us to deliver their curriculum in their way. Along with many other talented Aussie and Canadian teachers, I would laugh and cry at the craziness.

Desperate to find a way to make the difference I so believed in, I changed schools and tried to get on various promotion schemes—all to no avail. I was working in a system that is supposed to nurture and encourage, yet that very system held me back.

During this period, I even tried to leave education and go back to editing, but got short shrift in that industry too because I wasn't trained in England! Painful limiting echoes of earlier days in education.

Back in the classroom, I fought for opportunities and the right to take professional development courses to improve my leadership skills. I fought to do things my way rather than the system's way; the way I believed would provide young people with the best outcomes and chances for success. I questioned everything and annoyed many along the way.

It was exhausting going against the flow.

Working in the education sector quite simply wore me down. Eventually I gave up fighting and sought to fit in. I tried to meet the expectations of others.

In the end I learned to be average. I stopped speaking out and challenging. I lost my resilience. I no longer got interviews for the jobs I applied for. I chunked on weight because I was working such long hours and was too tired to eat properly. I no longer recognised the woman in the mirror. Worst of all I stopped believing in myself.

And then one insignificant-in-every-way day, a course on neuro-linguistic programming (NLP) floated across my computer screen. To this day, I have no idea what possessed me to go on that course. It was a course that changed my life.

I refer to NLP as my Canada. It gave me back positivity. It changed how I thought. It got me to let go of the rubbish that was holding me back. It got me to believe in myself again.

In just over a year, I studied to be an NLP trainer. I learned how to rewire my brain, see the world differently, and influence beliefs, choices and outcomes.

Then I took all that I had learned and applied it to a whole school! Yes, I was so inspired that I convinced the Headteacher to work differently--to spend time focusing on mindset rather than skills or content. He agreed, and not just with some staff or some students but with all staff and all students.

The results were amazing! It changed the way staff dealt with stress; how students dealt with adversity, and attendance and grades improved. We focused on the positives, the successes, the solutions, what was possible, what we could do instead of what we couldn't. Everyone benefitted.

I had found my authentic self again. Life was good again.

Until I received a letter telling me I was at risk of redundancy!

How dare they? After all I'd done, the hours I'd worked, the changes I'd made. But in just a short time, my new NLP-rewired brain kicked in and I started to consider the opportunity offered by the compensation package attached to redundancy.

Did I dare take this chance and walk away from a 20-year career when I could just hold my breath and collect my pension in a few years? I could actually feel the optimism rising at the idea of sharing what I had learned about how NLP can change your thinking with other women. If I could lead a change in culture and leadership style in one school, surely, I could do it elsewhere. If I could use my NLP skills to rewire my own brain to lose weight and regain my confidence, look younger and have tons more energy. then surely other women would want to benefit from that too?

I dared, I believed. In myself! I decided to go for it and start my own coaching and training business and I haven't looked back. I am in control of my life now. Instead of the old fears and doubts, I focus on the outcomes that I want. I have a clear goal and I am flexible as to how I achieve it.

As an entrepreneur, I have to hold on tight to that restored self-belief and reinforce it every day. I have quietened my inner critic and I practice gratitude for the awesomeness in my world. I have also surrounded myself with people who encourage me and believe in me and what is possible.

I truly believe I can do what I want to do in this world, and I believe you can too.

So, how exactly? Here are 3 suggestions that made a difference for me and could help you too.

1. Focus on what you want.

If you spend your energy and time thinking and worrying about the what ifs, the doubts, the criticisms, the problems, then that is what you will get. That's all you will see and you will miss the opportunities that present themselves to you.

This doesn't mean you shouldn't plan for anything that could sabotage your dream and it doesn't mean you ignore problems; it's just how you think about them.

Create a vision board for yourself. Put it on the wall or in a scrap book so you can inspire yourself every day. It will help your unconscious mind visualise what you want and increase the likelihood of it happening. Write out your goal - in great detail - as if you've already achieved it. Feel what it's like to be where you want to be!

See abundance, not lack. Be grateful for what is. Imagine what could be every single day.

2. Use positive language.

Language shapes our thoughts and feelings. Use positive words and phrases so that the impossible becomes possible.

When someone asks you how you are, choose "awesome", "amazing", "excellent." Send your mind in the direction you want to go.

Eliminate the word 'but' from your life as it automatically introduces doubt and defeat. Instead, use the word 'and' or find another way of saying what you want to say. For example, instead of thinking, " I'd like to work for myself, but I don't have any money," you could say, "I'd like to work for myself and I don't have any money right now so how can I get some?".

3. Change your critical inner voice.

Often that critical voice is so embedded and has been around for so long, we are no longer aware of what we're saying to ourselves that makes us doubt our abilities.

First, start becoming aware of your voice. Perhaps it tells you 'you're not as good as …' or argues 'what's the point?' Once you are aware, you can quieten or soften the voice - just turn down the dial. Change it to a voice that makes you laugh rather than cower, a voice that soothes instead of irritates, a voice that encourages rather than deflates.

That way the words of your inner voice will lose their power and eventually you will be able to change the words too to create a voice that believes in and supports you.

Bottom line? Empower yourself. Believe in yourself. Be the best version of you. Now!

Caroline Tyrwhitt is a mindset coach and NLP trainer; speaker and author of the forthcoming book 'The Mindset Diet'. She works one to one with busy professional women to help them lose weight and be their best selves again. Her great passion is working with female teachers to overcome self-doubt and overwhelm and lead with confidence and courage – to break through that inner glass ceiling and be the difference that makes the difference. You can connect with Caroline on Facebook and Linked In.

RIDING THE CAROUSEL

Round in circles, round I go;
Sometimes fast, sometimes slow.
How on earth will I ever know
That I've reached my destination?

Along the way, I experience signs,
Tiny touches, so divine.
A moment shared, a word, a lesson
An uplifting quote, someone's blessing.

Someone stops me to review,
Whispers "I believe in me; I believe in you."
I take a breather, drink in the view
Perhaps you relate, have been there too?

Yet, once again, mount the carousel,
My trusty steed knows this route so well.
And whilst we gallop gently to the music,
My sense of purpose, somehow, I lose it.

Ideas, ideas, swirl around,
Will I ever dismount this merry-go-round?
Multifaceted, magnificent, creatively inspired,
Yet not grounded, feeling "wired".

Now you've seen me, stilled the wheel,
Taken your place alongside on your saddle.
No more allow my genius to be concealed,
Thrown a lifeline; allowed to paddle.

Sue Williams

Inspiration Built on Intuition and Evolution

Cheryl Carey

"Feel the fear and do it anyway."
— Susan Jeffers

I𝑇'S NEARLY 11PM on the 16th December 2018. Tomorrow is the deadline to finish writing about 'one of my life experiences,' which will be worth completing if only to inspire at least one person.

Talk about leaving it to the last minute...often it is late at night when my creativity flows. It was the same with fashion designing years ago - mounds of paper flying and splayed around myself as I sat for hours conceiving ideas in my sanctuary on my bed!

I was particularly successful as a fashion and textile designer as I'm very creative due to my dyslexia, something I didn't find out about until I was 50 years old. When both of my daughters were diagnosed with dyslexia, the assessor offered to test me at the same time. Wow, what a bomb shell! Yet this diagnosis answered many questions and confirmed the cause of many obstacles. The diagnosis seemed to make it all ok and I felt I could be kinder to myself.

My daughters both have high IQ's, which meant I might also be clever! I felt a massive weight lift from my shoulders. I allowed myself time to adjust, accept and start to build my confidence. Along the way I realised I'd learnt many coping mechanisms; it was quite incredible and scary to think you could go so long in life battling something you didn't know existed.

After watching Sports Personality of the Year, featuring Billie Jean King, the famous female tennis player from the United States, I switched off the TV. She was certainly one of my favourite inspirational speakers and her final words struck a chord with me – "we all have a voice; we need to be heard." I took a gulp. This was not the first time I'd wanted to start to speak and write, thinking "is this it, is this the right time?"

With Billie Jean's words ringing in my ears, I finally faced my fear and decided to do it anyway – consciously – which is quite different to just doing it. Troubled thoughts swirled around my mind – "will I be judged, laughed at, feel humiliated, not be taken seriously or believed?" Perhaps I won't receive any recognition or acknowledgement, even if just for my participation and effort.

You see, it takes me twice as long to do this sort of thing. My dyslexia diagnosis explained a lot...

A little about me

I was married for 20 years to the Managing Director of an advertising agency with whom I had much in common. Yet, it felt like there was more to life. I wanted to grow and evolve, to be independent and travel. Forever willing and yearning to learn, I possessed a vivid imagination and zest for life; creativity and artistic tendencies. Very determined, I loved freedom. My big passions were hugely varied - people, animals, communication, nature, colour, design, sound: music – dance – chanting; travel, photography; my own way of experiencing religion and spirituality. I remember how, aged about 6 years old, I felt different to most people and my family. I was always labelled 'super sensitive' and have since learnt this is a gift of a healer and empath. Knowing all this, I took the difficult decision to leave my husband. Divorce followed months later, allowing me an opportunity to find my real authentic self.

I quite literally jumped in at the deep end, knowing it was going to be a bumpy ride, yet not quite realising the massive challenges I would face. And yes, I'm still pleased that I did.

I feel that I have brought up my two gorgeous daughters on my own over the last 25 years, without the benefit of any positive parenting from either of my own parents. I learnt from them what not to do, and I self-taught the hard way, by my experiences, with my own coping mechanisms and life skills. I learned from any mistakes I made along the way, whilst holding a deep 'knowingness' that things would work out. But this certainty was difficult to access at times, and I wished to learn more. That's how I became interested in self-development and taking responsibility for myself and all my actions and thoughts.

I went from rags to riches, then back to rock bottom again. Following the end of a second marriage which was abusive and controlling, I went out to work as a cleaner; successfully securing every job I went for. As I was only deemed to be as good as my last position, I did each one to the best of my ability. I found that people liked me because I was good, honest and trust-worthy.

I ended up doing more than cleaning, turning my services into a de-cluttering business, which I really enjoyed. One thing led to another - my communication and caring skills had become apparent - and people, friends and clients regularly came to me for help, support and advice. I chose to go back into education to reinvent myself, studying for a Master's degree in counselling, life coaching and several alternative therapies.

Much later, I went into the property market, in a small way, and ran a guest house, rental properties, a doggie hotel and events, amongst other things. I then experienced another life changing story as a 50 + single female, to whom the universe decides to offer another teaching...

A message from the universe

On one particular day in October 2017, I decided to attend a Friday ladies' talk at the last minute. On the way there in the car, I took a Bluetooth call from a colleague asking if I could accommodate one of her regular guests for 5 days and nights in my home, starting that very day. It was urgent as she had a dog who needed to stay with her. Caught unawares, I half agreed, and said that I would ring back after the lunch to confirm.

This did not follow my usual procedure as the decision was made quickly, without completing an online booking form. On returning the call, I offered to make a small detour on my way back to pick up the guest and the dog. When I arrived, I immediately recognised the house this new guest had been staying at, as it belonged to an old friend of mine. After I had picked up my new guest, I suggested for us to stop at the cash point so she could pay the costs of my accommodation. Her reply was "no"; she preferred internet banking.

Once she arrived at my place, I made a cup of tea and we had a friendly chat. I showed her the choice of bedrooms, and she chose the better of the two. During the next few days she was in and out all the while, at odd hours and with many shopping bags and the dog in tow.

By the end of the week I emailed requesting that full payment be made by 5 pm on Friday at the latest. To my shock, she took um-bridge at this!

The next thing I knew, a tall, bouncer-like man arrived at my front door using seriously threatening language and behaviour. I can say only that it was as if he was a character out of some action movie. He appeared to be completely 'out of it,' and menacing enough to make me think he could pull a knife! As you can imagine, at this point I felt incredibly scared, in real fear for my life. This huge man had been able to enter the house as he had been given the key by my female guest. I had to think rapidly on my feet, and quickly put in place a plan of action. I managed to keep him talking until I scrambled my way upstairs, where I hastily locked myself in my bedroom and rang for the police.

Then came my turning point...I knew I was being tested as I had been before in previous life-threatening situations. I realised that my sense of belief and trust had been weakened and that I had operated in a rushed manner trying to help someone else, to my detriment. My current situation was a very powerful reminder that I needed to regain my faith and trust my intuition once more! I prayed to God for help and protection also to Archangel Michael. I seriously will always 'believe and trust' and know that I am so well looked after and that I have courage, strength and trust in my intuition so as to be an inspiration for my daughters and others.

Quickly, I used my mobile phone to alert and delay friends and clients who were due to drop off their dogs for their weekend stay with me, as I didn't wish them to be caught up in all of this. They all ended up sat outside in the road watching events unfold and conversing with me via mobile to relay back his every move during the 15 minutes it took for the police to arrive. They caught the man and questioned him outside the house.

My hope is to leave a legacy that illustrates the importance of knowing when to say "no" - one of the words that has always been hardest for me to choose. Third time lucky – I have learnt so very much from this challenging situation.

Learning from experience

Although it is sometimes good to act spontaneously, it is not always sensible to rush into things without being prepared. Nowadays I take much more time to chill and relax and find that planning and organisation is often better. In retrospect, I recognise that the colleague who made the initial request was impatient. It had felt like she was trying to get this new client off her hands and over to mine as quickly as possible. On reflection, I should have been firm and said no, from the offset. Or at least, I could have taken time to go through my normal procedure, not doing so made it so much harder for myself.

I can be so keen to help. Perhaps you can relate? On this occasion, my automatic desire to be of service meant that I was too helpful too soon. I was inviting someone in to my home who I didn't know anything about, nor her dog! I didn't pause and listen to my intuition. Alarm bells had started to set in ... I was not the type of person who would usually take in or allow a stranger to stay with me in my home. This was compounded when she refused to make payment immediately, and then delayed and delayed. In retrospect, I can see that this was a big sign! Even the amount of shopping she brought with her seemed unusually excessive. I realise that this woman had no problem with putting herself first, now I know why she was really there.

This was a major turning point for me. Remembering how I had experienced other difficult situations over the years, I needed to take serious action - my life was in danger. An urgent reminder for me that it was extremely important to learn the lesson to trust in myself and my instincts again. This further opportunity was a blessing in disguise, meaning that I really did understand this time. I pleaded directly to God for help, knowing and trusting this would be ok. I needed a reminder of how I had done this on a few previous occasions with success. Archangel Michael is extremely strong, courageous, willing and quick to help and protect – he did just that.

I will never again doubt God, Archangel Michael, the Divine, the Universe, Source. This experience has given me my power back, even though it happened in such a dramatic way, it had to be, to help me realise that I am 'looked after.'

I will trust and believe always because of this very empowering experience.

My intuition is strong, clear, courageous, it nudges and speaks to me. I will always listen to it from now on, and truly wish my daughters and many others to benefit from my learnings, teachings and experiences.

What a gift, allowing me to expand mentally, physically and spiritually; enabling me to be more confident, stepping into my super powers, and noble-wisdom on this continual web of evolution.

My three tips to help everyone strengthen their self-belief, are:

1. Always believe in yourself and always trust your intuition and 'knowing', no matter how faint it sounds or feels; get clear. Meditation will help it to get stronger without questioning.

2. Own your own power and courage, never give it away.

3. Feel your fear and do it anyway.

Cheryl Carey was born in Cheshire, with two dysfunctional parents and two younger sisters. She attended a private all girls' school and went on to college to study Fashion Design and Textile Design. She met her first husband and moved into an idyllic village called Great Budworth and afterwards Arley, where she started her own fashion business. She later wound down the business to start a family, giving birth to two daughters, who she brought up alongside many pets. She divorced and remarried, to divorce again. Now living independently in Knutsford, running her businesses and always looking to develop herself further. Find out more at cherylcareyubique.weebly.com

I BELIEVE IT'S MY TIME

Why do I believe I'm so weak?
Why don't I just stand up and speak ?
Instead of acting like a freak
Outwardly appearing so meek
When inwardly my heart bleeds a leak.

Going along with the status quo
Doesn't really help my flow
Deploring myself for not
Having the power of my convictions,
Carry all life's contradictions.

Why be a 'goody goody'?
Doing what I don't want
Saps my strength
My energy
My peace

I Believe it's my time NOW

So, my dear the time has come
To get up and speak
Speak and be counted
Or otherwise
Remain dumbfounded.

Paramjit Oberoi

Reinvention

Chris Ramsbottom-Pampling

"What if I fall? Oh, but my darling, what if you fly?"
— *Erin Hanson*

O N THE 16TH of August 2012, I was told by the head cardiologist at my local hospital that, if I didn't stop taking the drugs the GP had prescribed for high blood pressure, I would be dead within three weeks. So, I stopped.

It had taken a year to get to the stage where my GP had referred me to a cardiologist because she thought I was in heart failure, and it took another year to get back to the stage where I felt I could return to some sort of work. I remember one day sitting in my home office, bored out of my tiny mind, and shouting at the wall, "OK universe; I'm ready – what can I do next?"

Really, it all started at the end of 2014 when I was chewing the fat with a friend. "So, Chris, what are your goals for 2015 then?" he said. Gently, I explained that I don't do this goal-setting stuff. Being born with two deformed kidneys, having five miscarriages and getting the familial dose of rheumatoid arthritis, I had had enough of setting myself up to fail by setting goals that my recalcitrant body decides I can't achieve.

It was what Dave said next that was the key. It was almost as if he'd opened a wormhole to the future. "What would you say, if you knew that just by saying it, it would happen?" And from thin air, I heard myself saying "I'd open a therapy centre."

The next thing I said was "Where the **** did that come from?"

It was not what I anticipated saying at all. It was not on my radar. I had given up all thoughts of having my own place, ever since having to leave a former centre, Utopia in Warwick in 2009 because my landlady hadn't paid her landlord. So, taking everything into consideration, I decided to ignore what I'd just said.

A few days later, I was leaving my bank and happened to look up at the first floor of the building opposite, where for the first time I saw a To Let sign. "That's interesting," I thought. A couple of days later, I'd gone down with the annual lurgy and, to save myself from getting too bored, I decided to google the property.

Well, it was about twice as big as I needed, but then I thought, I could let the other rooms out, and the rent was reasonable. So, I put an enquiry in and waited.

The next day the landlord rang. He asked me what I wanted to do with the building. I told him I wanted to put a therapy centre there. You could have knocked me down with a feather when he told me he wanted to do that too! But he was a builder who didn't want to deal with multiple therapists. He just wanted to deal with one person. Me.

Then I had a dream.

As I walked through the door, my heart sank. I knew exactly where I was. I knew the faded, dingy wallpaper: the outdated furniture: the dirty curtains. I knew the layout like the back of my hand – after all, I had spent so much time here, they even gave me my own room, number 419. Oh yes. This was Hell.

The women I arrived with sat around the table. I addressed them: "Ladies, do you know where you are?" Most of them shook their heads, but Pam, an older lady with grey hair in waves, said: "Oh yes, we're in Hell!" This obviously came as a shock to most of them; in fact, the youngest screamed and ran towards the exit.

"Don't stop her," I said. "There is only one way out, and that's The Abyss. All there is, is you – and The Abyss. You fall for lifetimes, and then you stop and then – nothing. Well, last time, I landed on my head, and I'm not doing that again! I'm sure there's another way out. "Pam, are you with me? Look, I'm going to find this other way, but Pam I want you to get that phone off the wall and dial 419 and invite whoever answers to join us."

I grabbed my red bag and walked in the opposite direction to the Exit sign, while Pam got the ancient wall phone and dialled. I could see a huge glass wall, through which you could see clouds and blue sky, but just at the side of it was a tiny wooden door. That was the one. So, I returned to the other ladies. There were fewer of them than I'd left, but Pam was still there.

A few minutes later, we were joined by a man with thinning blonde hair, piercing blue eyes and a troubled expression. "Hello, I'm Allan," he said. Now, this was not what I was expecting, so I said to Pam, "Did you ring 419?" "Oh no, I think it was 418." I sighed and turned to Allan, muttering "I suppose he'll do then." "Do you know where you are?" I asked. "Oh yes, I'm in Hell," he said. "Are you up for finding the other way out?" "Well, yes," he said. I addressed them all. "Now look everyone, I've found the other way out. You're quite welcome to stay here, to use the Exit if you want, or you can follow me. But I'm going through the Other Door."

With that, I picked up my red bag and walked towards the tiny door, which was growing larger by the second. I looked around and saw that only Pam was with me, the others were still sitting in stunned silence. Allan was holding the door open for me. I walked through the door, into the light…

… and looked around. I was on Ball Hill in Coventry. Allan was standing in front of me, his wings clearly visible. "Well done! You made it out of Hell. But there is a payment you must make. Your payment, Chris, is to enable other people to escape from Hell too. It doesn't matter whether it is for ten minutes or a lifetime – but you must do it." And with that, he touched the roller shutter marked "Amethyst Centre" and opened the door. I saw a staircase going upwards into golden light. "Good luck," said Allan. And upwards I went.

So that is how it all started. When you are doing what you are on this earth to do, the universe moves itself to facilitate it, and that is exactly what has been happening. I heard a radio broadcast which said that 56-year-old women had been taking their personal pensions to start businesses, and so I decided to investigate doing just that. I had two tiny personal pensions, and if I'd let them mature, I'd just about have enough for one bag of groceries per month if I was lucky. Put them together however and I had enough for the Amethyst Centre to happen. I handed the landlord the required amount with just two days to spare!

This is the point of the song quote at the start. If I'd have stopped at "But I might fall," I'd never have dreamed this amazing place into being. Instead, I believed in the "What if you fly?" part, and I decided to give it a go. Thank God I did!

My tips to support the growth of self-belief:

1. Recognise that you don't know everything, despite having made it to fifty years old!

2. Recognise that you don't have to know everything.

3. Sometimes, you have just got to trust that there is a higher power at work and that it has your back. If you need wings, you will get them – but not before you take that leap!

Chris Ramsbottom-Pampling realised when she was 28 that nobody, least of all a man, was going to make her life happy. It was something she had to do for herself. So, she left her first husband for her second husband and moved Up North. She doesn't regret this for a moment: she was able to train as a teacher of adults, something she'd wanted to do for years. She was also adopted by cats at this time. However, at the turn of the century, she became aware that she had the chance to rectify an error, and so she left her 2nd husband for her 3rd husband. No more husbands! Life has taken several turns, all for the best since then. The last one is detailed above. www.amethystcentre.com

I BELIEVE

My poems
My story
My precious past
My present predicament
Each have a story to tell
Of predicted pain inflicted

I Believe

Poems truly reflect psyche powers
Permeating through every pulsating cell
They each have a story to tell
You cannot force; neither compel

I Believe

Poems restore; pour out the past
Puncture the inflated ego
Help to explore
The depths
The paths
The heights
The slights
All conditions to which I have been submitted

I Believe

You can't force or compel
Thoughts.
Nothing flows for days;
Pulsating cells burst
Spew feelings;

Every touch
The urge to clutch
Tight and write and write

I Believe

Poems purposefully open
The path to
Propagating goodness

Paramjit Oberoi

How Cricket Helped Me to Find the Path to my *Solo Success!*

Christine Ingall

"Happiness is not a goal: it's a by-product."
— Eleanor Roosevelt

T HIS IS A story about how strength, resilience and self-worth can grow from neglect and the impact it has through hurt, anger and pain. How it is possible to flip the negative and find instead the positive results.

Imagine a beautiful garden that gradually over time is not watered or tended by the person who is supposed to care for it. Weeds start to take over the flower beds, vegetable patch and pathways. But the seeds of the wild flowers among the weeds also grow and thrive at the same time. Eventually, in what appears to be an overgrown and neglected piece of land, the wildflowers bloom and proliferate to create their own new pathway through the chaos.

Beginnings

In the 1978 number 1 hit *Dreadlock Holiday* by the group 10cc, there's a catchy chorus that starts, "I don't like cricket. I *love* it!" Well, before I had a relationship with someone who played cricket, I didn't realise that cricket-love could be a sporting all-consuming passion. Nor that it would be the catalyst to spark the beginning of the end of our relationship. And, for me, it would also be the beginning of my journey into acquiring the confidence, skills and experience required to live a solo life, and make a success of it. Such a success, in fact, that I was able to write a book about it.

We met, the cricketer and I, on the first day of my first job in London. He had the most beautiful, mellifluous speaking voice I had ever heard. (He was proper, public school, posh.) I was thrilled to be quickly absorbed into the after-work socialising of my new and fascinating colleagues – all in their twenties like me - including the cricketer. We gradually got to know each other, in and out of the office, over the course of a year, even though he had a steady girlfriend and I had lots of dates.

We apparently each thought the other 'a catch', and got together at Christmas. By the time the cricket season started months later, we were in love. That summer, I recall a few weekends when I accompanied him and the team to an away match and watched my beloved's heroics on the pitch and in the outfield. But however much I tried, I couldn't maintain an interest in whether he actually had his leg in front of the wicket; was run out for an embarrassingly low score; or achieved an amazing catch to get someone out. I went along to spend lazy afternoons in the sunshine, chatting with the team wives and girlfriends, munching on finger-food and then going to the post-match booze-up (regardless of whether our team had won) in the local pub.

Over successive seasons I learnt a great deal about cricket and those who play the game. But I wasn't really interested in the cricket to be honest. It was HIS game, so I supported him in whatever way I could: I knitted him a cricket pullover with a cable pattern; I let him wash his cricket whites in my washing machine; I listened along with him to the cricket commentary on the car radio. This appeared to be mainly about cake and whatever had stopped play. But was often eye-wateringly funny as in, "The batsman's Holding the bowler's Willie." The gods of cricket have a sense of humour.

Daily living

We were a couple but never lived together. When I bought a flat, he didn't move in with me. But he always stayed at mine, with me, from Friday night to Monday morning. Sometimes we also saw each other in the week with mutual friends for celebrations, or to visit his mum and other family members. This arrangement suited us: we had free evenings to socialise with our own friends and new colleagues as we changed jobs and our careers progressed.

I no longer wanted to go to the weekend cricket match. One game of cricket, usually on a Sunday, wasn't a game-changer in our relationship. I always saw him after the match - he came back afterwards to mine, or I joined him at the pub and we then went home (to mine) together. Anyway, I had a large social circle, lots of interests and was never short of something to do, especially when I had a new flat to decorate and furnish.

A cricket widow

After about five years together things started to change cricket-wise and impact more on the time that we had together all year round. 'Winter nets' – indoor practice pitches for bowlers and batters were frequented outside the season. Then during the season, he had opportunities to play two games each weekend. I suggested that I (and other partners) might go along for the ride for one of the two games, every now and then. But it was too far, there were too many of us, too much match kit luggage and not enough cars, or no train station as the village was in the back of beyond, or any number of reasons… So, I left it to him to decide whether he would play both games. He usually chose to play.

I started to suspect that he was literally playing away (having an affair) during at least one of these matches. However, he usually came back to mine after a match: I basically owned the flat he slept in at the weekends. And I mean slept. This didn't alleviate my suspicions. One way or another, cricket was dominating our relationship and I had become a cricket-widow – even if only in my mind.

So, what did I do with all this extra time on my hands? I was used to seeing my friends out and about in London, for meals, a show, an exhibition or a film on at least one day of the summer cricket season weekend. But it was usually in the daytime/early evening as I arranged things around the returning cricketer. I realised how much I resented the way I had let his hobby dominate my life. So, I started to arrange to do things with them at other times: a show in the evening; a party going on till late - well early morning; dinner rather than lunch.... I didn't know what time I would get home; it would probably be late; he might as well go back to his flat.

But mindful of our problems, I completed an evening massage course in the hope that I could inject something new into, and restart our love-life – when we were actually in an intimate setting.

Going solo

And I began to do things on my own, rather than make arrangements with other people all the time. Sometimes I didn't fancy the film they wanted to see. I chose to go to my nearest cinema and see something else. Or I wanted to see an exhibition on the last available day for me to see it before it closed. Or I wanted to do something new, something different that I'd never done before. Or explore a different part of London or a new development that everyone was talking about. I was passionate about the theatre and started to go to as many shows as I could fit into each week and weekend. I chose what I would do in my spare time. I started to operate independently of the cricketer, regardless of whether he was playing one match or two at the weekend.

It was easier to do all these things alone in London rather than anywhere else. In the big city you are somehow more inconspicuous, or at least it felt like that. But I still had to learn to walk over the threshold of the cinema, the theatre, the museum, alone; to brace myself to ask for one ticket; a table for one; a single glass of wine. To enroll onto and regularly attend a massage techniques course in a different part of London, without anyone to spur me on and without knowing if there would be any reward at the end. (There wasn't.) Somehow, everything was more intimidating and I felt judged being on my own surrounded (or so it felt) by loved-up couples.

However, I talked to and went for coffee with strangers I met in a gallery or the theatre bar. God, after all, I was desperate for attention! I needed someone to twinkle at me and laugh at my jokes. I could have gone on dates. I learned a lot about keeping safe and grew in confidence.

I laughingly told the cricketer about my adventures – but he didn't know how to respond. By the time he started to ask if I wanted to go to a weekend match with him, or he was suddenly free because rain prevented play, I had already made plans. But I wanted us to stay together and always tried to work around those plans and make time for him, even though I felt he hadn't done the same for me.

The writing is on the wall

It was too late. We had a problem relationship in which we were making each other unhappy, even as we tried to put things right. The writing was on the wall for us and I knew what it said. Getting to the 'last over' took some time and lots of soul searching. When it came, we were both heartbroken. After all, we had been in love. We still *loved* each other, exemplified in our unbroken loving relationship, seeing each other regularly for many years afterwards. I last saw him 20 years ago and wish him well always.

This is where I admit that I wasn't Miss Perfect! We both had problems (more than/as well as cricket) that I don't need to go into. But I always think of cricket as being the wedge that came between us and, eventually, drove us apart. If it hadn't, I would never have discovered the challenge and joys of learning to do things on my own. I was able to cope full-time on my own when the relationship ended, and I was single again. (I did search for Mr. Right, but he was elusive.)

Solo lifestyle skills

Anyway, I carried on living alone, and without a partner while working in London, then through job moves to Sheffield and finally to Leamington Spa. Throughout all that time, I learned how to *live* alone and not go mad; how to ward off loneliness; how to start again in a new city or town knowing no-one; how to be brave enough to find and pursue the things that made me happy - singing, acting, being creative. I was unconsciously honing and developing the attitude and skills for a solo life that I started to learn while I went through a relationship break up.

In the 1990s when my mum's partner died, she found herself living alone for the first time in her life, and struggled. She turned to me for support and advice, and I realised that she regarded me as an expert. But it wasn't until I was in my 50s that I realised that I possessed an unusual skillset that wasn't acknowledged in society. And there could be people, like my mum, struggling with doing things alone and also feeling lonely.

Although I had always been a writer and documented my life in many ways, it took me 30 years of living alone to realise that my experience and expertise could be the basis of a book. I wrote my self-help guide *Solo Success! You CAN do things on your own* for people who were living alone, not in a romantic relationship and made to feel like a failure in our couple-centric society. I wanted to help and encourage all those people - 7.7 million people in the UK and rising. Now I am a champion of and commentator on the solo lifestyle: how to be **SOLO,** lead a better solo life and not be apologetic about it. I hope I have, in some way, succeeded. Most people will need to know how to be successfully solo at some point in the future.

Exercises

Here are a few tips to help, if you want to try doing some things on your own and need to build up your confidence. Whatever you do and wherever you go, remember you have the same right to be there as everyone else. And think of all the things you will have to talk about!

1. Add doing something on your own to a chore or task that you do regularly. For example, go for a tea/coffee after doing the supermarket shopping and before going home. Most large chain supermarkets have a café, or call into a favourite one that is on the way home. If you want to make sure you will have someone to talk to, check if there is a Chatty Café in your area, usually one of the Costa group, where there will be a designated table for people on their own to drink and chat. (www.thechattycafescheme.co.uk)

2. Go to places that you know because you go there, or have been there, with family and/or friends, as the surroundings will be familiar to you. You will know, for example, whether the seating is comfortable, if food is served, where the loos are, if there is a garden. And whenever you will be sitting at a table for one, take something with you to read or otherwise keep you from staring at other people.

3. Set a 'solo event date' with yourself to do something special on your own once a month. Check what's on in your area and book a ticket to see a film or play, hear a concert, attend an exhibition or take a daytrip to a country house, garden or museum. Something that YOU want to do.

Christine Ingall is the author of *Solo Success! You CAN do things on your own*, a top-ten Amazon bestseller in its category available in paperback and e-book formats. She is a writer, speaker and **weekly** blogger (Twitter and Facebook) on the solo lifestyle and related issues and writes the **monthly** Solo Supplement for Psychologies Magazine's online 'Life Labs' section. She is regularly interviewed for radio programmes and has a number of press articles published.

www.https:/psychologiesmagazine/lifelabs/solosupplement

www.cjiwrites.com/blogs

ANYTHING IS POSSIBLE

You took your first tentative steps as a young child,
Coped with the inevitable stumbles along the way;
Instinctively relied upon those around you
Who picked you up and soothed tears after each fall.

Despite early difficulties you found practice made perfect,
Until eventually you stood on your own two feet.
Your confidence grew; independence was a wonderful feeling!

Although life may not always be the easiest of journeys,
Goals and choices sometimes need to be adjusted to fit;
If you can remember that earliest sense of achievement
There's really nothing which cannot be within your reach

Diane Durham

Uncovering the Clues
in Your Life Story

Daphne Radenhurst

"The privilege of a lifetime is to become who you really are."
— Carl Jung

MY LIFE IS rather like a detective story. Looking back, the first part was like a movie, lived through me by other people. I began to take control in the second part, using skills of detection and self-exploration to discover life's possibilities for myself. Now, aged 91, I have attained a large measure of self-understanding, yet still have more to learn.

Right from the start, it seemed there was a surplus of mystery in my life.

The story begins in Paris. While studying art, my mother discovered she was pregnant after fleeing a relationship with a married man in Toronto. Then, I was born in Nice. Why Nice? I don't know. Looking at the evidence, perhaps my mother was advised to go to the English clinic there, by a well-meaning friend. Did my mother want me? Again, I don't know. Yet, it must have been hard to get rid of an unwanted baby back then...

Fortunately, my mother had some money and France was inexpensive then. I remember the warmth of my mother's love, her ample bosom, and her comforting presence.

When I was three, we moved to Brittany to live in a convent pension run by Catholic nuns. An ideal place for children. A path led from the convent to the beach, a sheltered cove with soft yellow sand and shallow water. I was in and out of the sea all the time, I made sandcastles and jumped down onto the sand from the low wall. The nuns were kind, the food was good, and the place was filled with happy, pre-war families.

All this changed in 1932, when my mother lost her money in the financial crash caused by the world Depression. Penniless, she had to find work. Out of a sense of their Christian charity the nuns promised to look after me, now 4 years old.

What a strange story! Could this happen today? I think not. I would be taken into care, put into a home, fostered, who knows what?

The question arises, was I happy? My skills of deduction lead me to believe that initially, I must have been devastated at being separated from my mother. While not exactly recalling these feelings, I have proof in drawings I made in an art therapy course many years later. The drawings show black bars with flames of fire, a crying child, and menacing black figures around me.

Out of necessity, I must have become used to the nuns and settled into their orderly life of prayers, services and worship. This included chanting and bells. I do remember the bells. I used to process solemnly round the garden with them, telling the beads on my own little rosary and reciting the Hail Mary.

Evidence suggests that I turned into a little nun. My love of order and neatness sprang from that time, and other characteristics such as feelings of guilt; that the body was something of which to be ashamed. I especially felt that I was unworthy.

Not wanting me to be brought up a Catholic, my mother removed me from the convent aged seven. Too young to process all these events, I think I was a thoroughly mixed up little girl.

We came to England, where my mother found work as a cook/housekeeper in a boarding school. Here I must pause to praise my mother. All her life she worked unstintingly to make a living for us both and to ensure I received a good education.

Yet, sadly, we grew apart. The bond between us, already broken by those years at the convent, became more marked. I was a bookworm, a bit of a nerd with strong mystical leanings. My mother was an intelligent, practical woman with a great interest in politics, but no interest whatsoever in spiritual matters. I felt unable to confide in her about any of my problems during my adolescence.

A shy girl, unable to make any real friends, my unusual background meant that I turned into a loner, a 'maverick' as someone once described me. I did well in school and went to university. It was at university that I used my questioning skills to explore why I was as I was. I read books by Jung, Freud and Adler, gaining an inkling that the cause of my problems lay in childhood. However, any kind of psychological treatment was too expensive, and so there the matter rested.

Whilst at university, I had a first glimpse of Paris. Travelling to a five-week summer school in San Sebastian, Spain we drove through Paris to change train stations. It was my 21st birthday. My first time back in France since childhood, I was entranced by Paris and the French people, and I responded to it with every fibre of my being. That strong sense of place and memory stayed with me through the following years, even as I secured a first-class degree and launched myself onto the London scene. I did so with disastrous results.

I formed a relationship with a 'mad' artist and searched for work. Without confidence and no skills apart from my academic studies, I was sorely qualified for any kind of practical employment. I moved from one unsatisfactory job to another.

The 'mad' artist ended up in an institution. Alarmed, my mother removed me from London. We moved to Cornwall, where I met one of my dearest friends, Kate Tilley, manageress of the Lobster Pot hotel in Mousehole, where I was installed as the receptionist.

Tall and glamorous, the sister of Kenneth More, the film star, Kate was outgoing and had great warmth. She was also very intuitive and able to see through the defences I had built over the years. Taking me under her wing, she became my confidante and greatest ally; rather like my own Doctor Watson who supported me and encouraged me in everything I did. We remained firm friends till she died at the age of ninety-nine and I scattered her ashes from the end of the harbour in Mousehole, in the Cornwall that she dearly loved.

In 1959, fate intervened. I applied successfully for a job with NATO in Paris and moved there with my mother. I felt that one of my dreams had finally come true! However, another legacy of my illegitimate birth was that I had no nationality, and I could not stay in France without a passport. Here again, fate took a turn, and the powers that be in NATO intervened to assist me in becoming a naturalised British citizen.

During thirty years with NATO, our financial situation gradually improved; enabling us to rent a flat and buy our own furniture. I learnt to drive and bought a car. Mother lived with me until she died, aged 88. Never close, we shared fairly amicably, both needing each other in our different ways. Now, in my old age, I look on her with great respect and affection.

Over the years, I had a nervous breakdown and recurring bouts of depression. In 1970 I found an esoteric school of philosophy, I think of it as a 'wisdom school' which set me on a spiritual path, which I believe saved my life and prevented me from spiralling on a downward path.

The 'School' as we called it, restored me to the belief in a Creator. Largely based on Hindu philosophy, it struck a chord within me. Like detectives, we learnt to examine our thought processes. I was stunned to discover how negative mine were! Following the clues led me to see that I was literally digging a hole in the ground for myself.

We were taught how to practice mindfulness and shown how to conserve our energy by pausing between activities. We learned about the three 'gunas' or energy principles – rajas, tamas and sattva – loosely being the energy of action, of inaction and the still centre between them. We were also initiated into the spiritual practice of Transcendental Meditation. Since that time, I have followed a spiritual path, and have found a practice of meditation invaluable.

I was now in my early 50s and learnt about the higher self, through the teachings of the School and began to develop a much more positive self-image. After my mother's death I fell in love for the first time in my life, and my whole emotional landscape began to expand. I was offered a new job, and I moved from a back-room office to a front office where I was able to use all my talents and skills.

I stayed on at NATO until my retirement in 1989, fortunate to work for a man I greatly admired, ultimately feeling happy and fulfilled in my work. He evidently appreciated me as he recommended me to receive the Member of the Order of the British Empire (MBE).

Upon retirement, I returned to England, deepening my detective skills by availing myself of many opportunities for self-help. I studied the therapeutic methods of Psychosynthesis, where I learned about my "inner child," explored what it meant to be fatherless and began to understand myself better.

On a trip to India in 1993, I had a remarkable experience in the ashram of Ramana Maharshi. I received two clear messages in the deep silence of the meditation room: "See the divine flame in every being" and "Drop your mental baggage." Like Holmes, I have pondered on those two messages ever since.

This experience transported me into a space of timelessness and complete joy, which lasted for days. However, back in England, I fell into a deep black hole of depression. By now, I sought to understand my depression, not hiding it by taking pills. I started seeing a therapist, a Buddhist psychosynthesis practitioner who helped me to climb out of the hole.

I started to paint - a source of great joy to me, and began to sing with Gilles Petit, a dynamic Frenchman who taught us the Indian way of raga singing. I discovered that I had a voice, and I enjoyed the exploration of the hundreds of different ragas, suitable to different times of the day. I refined my powers of listening and began to appreciate music more deeply.

Life gradually settled down. I achieved a measure of contentment in my small house with a garden, my first 'home'. I never had the happiness of finding a partner or having a family, and in some respects my life has been somewhat lonely, although I have many good friends.

Several years ago, I joined the International Association for Conscious and Creative Writers, founded by Julia McCutchen, and began writing my life story. I got to know a number of talented, amazing women, now close friends and writing buddies. I enjoy a wonderful, supportive online network of friends and colleagues. As someone who lives on their own, this is one of the very positive aspects of the internet.

The final step of my investigative journey saw my return to the Abbaye in Brittany, where I lived my most formative years. An incredible experience for me, it is here that I have rediscovered my childhood. Although modernised, the exterior of the building remains the same, much as I remember it. The beauty of the surrounding landscape - the sea, outlying islands and rocks, the outgoing tide exposing the mud and sand where people still go foraging for whelks and mussels, reminiscent of my time there over 80 years ago. Untouched by tourism, it still retains an almost mystical sense of a place where heaven and earth meet.

Above all, the same spirit remains there, created by centuries of prayer, worship and devotion to a higher purpose. No longer a convent; now a thriving hub of encounter, intellectual and creative pursuits and a retreat centre where people find peace and refuge away from our busy world.

Returning home from this happy place, I felt my spirits slowly eroding away until I found myself in a very dark place. Once more I had to question myself. What was this telling me? With the help of a Life Coach I explored this final stage of my journey. Finally, in an extraordinary sharing with two spiritual friends, I was able to make sense of my experience, relate it to my time in the ashram, and bring together and integrate the light and the shadow in my psyche. I am now whole. I realise that all the inhibitions that held me back have dropped away. I am free to be myself. I have truly come home.

I feel my journey has been one of discovery, of searching for the clues that hold the answer to this strange story that has been my life. I don't hold conventional religious beliefs, but I do believe in a higher source, and in the power of love.

So, aged 91, I am ready to face whatever life still has to throw at me! I am prepared to finally complete my mysterious life story. I believe I have uncovered the final piece of revelation I was searching for. I give thanks for the gifts I have been given to navigate this extraordinary life of mine, and to bring it finally into safe harbour.

Three of the practices that have helped me are:

- Meditation practice. I believe it has kept me on an even keel, balanced and in equanimity through most of the vicissitudes of my life, and also accounts for my good health into an advanced age. The physical benefits of meditation are well known, and even more so the spiritual benefits.

- The sounding practice which uses the Indian tonal scale, SA RE GA MA PA DA NI SA. Whenever I feel out of kilter, I start to chant these notes, and in a very short time I am back in my centre again. I can play with these notes and create my own song, my soul song.

- My writing practice, that which is closest to my heart. I use the continuous writing practice, just pouring everything out onto the page, or the more conscious writing practice.

Daphne Radenhurst is a linguist, poet, writer, artist and singer. Separated from her mother at the age of four for four years, and living with nuns, she has experienced periods of black depression alternating with periods of enlightenment. It has been her lifelong quest to examine these states of mind in an objective and forensic manner. In her 20s she wrote: ''My aim is to sing a song of beauty.'' Now at the age of 91 she has published her book: *The Heroine's Journey* to inspire and enlighten others. Daphne's blog is: michousgarden.com

VOICE IT!

I have a voice,
I have a choice,
Whether to speak,
Sing, chant, rejoice.
Hear my sound,
So profound,
Echo joyfully
Around my ribcage,
Reverberate; ricochet.

Slay the demons,
Beat down the door,
This is what my voice is for!
Hallelujah, found at last,
Previously felt forever held back,
Stuck under a morass of Elastoplast!
Sing out, loud and proud,
Ethereal, athletic, profound the sound
No longer going underground.

Sue Williams

When Life Calls for a Life Jacket

Debrah Goldston

"Breathe, darling
This is just a chapter,
It's not your whole story"
— *S C Lourie*

IT SEEMS TO me that life is rather like interior decorating; we all know that better results are achieved if we strip back to the bare surfaces before repainting. So, why is the temptation to simply slap on more paint often so great? Perhaps the answer lies in our fear of being exposed, both to others and, most importantly, to ourselves. Yet it is my opinion that it is only through a thorough and deliberate stripping back to the bare essence of ourselves that we will ever bring our new and exciting life chapter into existence. My story is about how I was nudged and eventually pushed by the universe into what can only be described as the refurbishment of my life!

Have you ever felt like your path was set? Your boat is surely heading along the river in an almost pre-determined direction. You are certain about life, even smug. Then it happens: the tsunami named life heads directly at you and, in what seems like a moment, everything is washed away.

That moment for me coincided more or less with my 50th birthday. Thank you, universe, for inviting the roller coaster named menopause to the party. Of course, the reality is probably that life's events are always inextricably linked, and the turmoil of hormonal transition fuelled the sequence of events leading me to identify with Queen Elizabeth's' "annus horribilis" or, in my own words, "the shittiest year of my life."

I separated from my husband after nearly two decades together and moved into a new home, alone. Six weeks later, it was catastrophically flooded, and I lost virtually every physical possession. In the midst of this, my Mum had a heart attack and my Dad became seriously ill. The life that I had known was literally washed away and only piles of mud remained. Curiously, or not, my home was the only property in the village to be affected. The floodwater was foul and the residual gunk smelly. Interesting symbolism!

Ask many people who experience their own version of what has long since been referred to as "the dark night of the soul" and afterwards (but rarely during), they will all tell you the same thing: that they are glad it happened. So, I wonder: is the world filled with masochists or is there really a deep and profoundly healing journey hidden within such trauma and painful experience? I believe that the "success' or otherwise of what happens next in the life of anyone finding themselves in this position may hinge on this very question.

So, what do you do when surrounded by the ruins of your former life? Options certainly exist: get in bed and stay there, for one. Tempting as this first choice can be, it leads only to waste and regret. That's not to say that, for me, a handful of days spent indulging my own deep sense of victimhood didn't have its place, because it did, but after that, the road to healing lay rather in the somewhat bolder choice of surrender.

Surrender to what? I hear you ask. Surrender to the feelings and emotions that arise from being right here, right now, in this moment and allowing ourselves to feel vulnerable, victimised, betrayed, unworthy and absolutely any other emotion that this experience evokes. Becoming fully aware of how we feel opens the door to profound healing. Awareness is everything. When we allow ourselves to be aware and vulnerable, we are inevitably no longer in denial or resistance; we just are.

As an empath and highly sensitive soul, I had spent years shielding myself from my feelings, but once the deluge had occurred, I could no longer sustain the pretence. This is where true, lasting change and soul growth finally becomes possible. We face ourselves fully in the mirror at last, no longer unwilling to see who we are, warts and all.

Up until that point, I now realise that I was a metaphysical and spiritual teacher and coach who was ashamed to admit her own failings and didn't know how to be vulnerable or accept that she didn't have all of the answers. For many, including me, it is at this critical point, when we finally declare that we cannot go on like this and ask the universe for help that, as if by magic, finally the big shift and transformation of our lives can occur. We, get out of our own way at last.

Of course, the transformation is rarely instant. Sometimes, it seems, the answers are like seeds that require planting and the right conditions, nurturing and time, in order to flourish into solutions and new ways of being in the world. Those working with the land will happily tell you that crops also need rotating and sometimes even burning back to stubble at the roots in order to bare optimal results. There is a reason why the expression is "phoenix rising from the ashes" and not "phoenix rising from my super comfortable life where everything is ticking along nicely." There is no real growth or expansion in the comfort zone.

So, I recommend being always on your guard for your comfort zone. This is the domain of the ego, a place where any level of soul atrophy is still preferable to change. The ego is interested only in one thing, namely survival. To this end, it will select and sustain unhappiness, misery, severe ill health and even death rather than allow the growth that our higher self demands. Conflict and lack of alignment are the results. Healing and lasting change simply will not occur in this state of being.

During such a pivotal time in the souls' maturation, it is also essential to be patient and ask the universe for help, remain positive, nurture the physical body with good nutrition, ensure adequate rest and maintain loving thoughts, especially towards oneself. However, this seems to be particularly difficult for women.

Without wishing to reinforce any stereotypical gender labels, I have observed through many years of clinical work as well as with myself, that women have a challenging time in prioritising themselves. This is especially so when they are mothers. The classic response from ourselves and often those around us, is that we are being selfish whenever we prioritise our own needs above all else. However, if you have ever been on an aircraft, you will be familiar with the standard safety demonstration, which instructs passengers, in the event of an emergency situation, to fit their own oxygen masks before helping others. The message is clear: we help no one when we have already lost consciousness ourselves.

My personal experience during this time involved a series of tiny bite size shifts in my behaviour and thinking. I reduced my working hours in order to create more "me time" and made a conscious effort to meet up socially with family and friends more frequently. I created space for walking in the countryside and for simple pleasures such as cuddling my pet cats. This process really brought home to me that the adage about the simple things in life having most meaning was entirely true. Up until this point, I was a workaholic and honestly felt that there was nothing wrong with working incredibly hard, seven days every week. As I relaxed into a simpler and quieter life, I was so busy enjoying a slower pace that I didn't even mind the lower income that less work initially brought about.

I fully appreciate how challenging it can be to erase a life time of familial, cultural and even religious programming regarding issues such as the need to work hard and, especially, the role of the feminine, always to nurture and take care of the home and all who reside there. For our generation, quite often this role has been further expanded into providing peer support, some form of charitable or other community contribution and even that of a matriarchal figurehead in the workplace. My staff even used to call me "Mum" and I was oblivious to the warning signs inherent in this.

My own experience and that of many women who I work with professionally, is that being a competent and reliable woman often results in more being asked of us by others. Identified as a safe and dependable pair of hands, who is always available, always kind and generous with both our time and our energy, it is all too easy for us to continually give to others until we have little left for ourselves. Finding time for the self in such an environment is tricky but must become a focus, if we are not just to survive but to flourish and become the best version of ourselves.

Saying "no" was hard for me at first but, as with many things in life, became easier with lots of practice. I began with small refusals and gradually made my way to bigger ones. Perhaps ironically, it is when we do finally prioritise our own wellbeing, that we are in a position to make a real and valuable contribution to the external world. Everyone benefits when we are at our best.

So where am I now, as a result of all of the challenges that I faced back then? The honest truth is that I still face challenges, some small and some more significant. This is life and, for those committed to their own soul evolution, the healing process is ongoing.

However, I am wiser and stronger and much more content, most of the time anyway. I have learned that hardship is transitory, and sadness passes. I allow myself to feel whatever is there in my heart and to be vigilant to my thoughts, but I finally appreciate too that my feelings and thoughts are not me and I always have a choice as to how I behave. Instead of being triggered by life's events, I use them as a means by which to explore who I am and to make revisions where I desire a different way forward. So, I am glad that all this happened to me, but that's easy to say now!

The following 3 simple exercises are suggested ways of connecting to your own version of the wisdom contained in this chapter:

Exercise 1

Building self-awareness

Every day and preferably several times every day, stop for a moment and ask yourself "what am I feeling right now?" Then simply be aware of the response, without editing or otherwise interfering with what comes up.

This simple but highly effective practice becomes second nature usually within just a few days of repeated practice and it is surprising what insights you will receive. Simply by giving ourselves permission to feel and acknowledging those feelings, we can begin to set ourselves free from years of bottled up emotions and self-denial.

Exercise 2

Breaking free from resistance.

Universal law dictates: that which you resist, persists. This exercise is therefore an invitation to give up the habit of resisting yourself. Once you have been practicing exercise one for a short time and your inner feelings and emotions begin to emerge, you are then in a position to surrender to them, instead of resisting them. This can be achieved through simple acknowledgment, with an intention of surrender and acceptance. An example might be "even though XYZ, I still dearly love and accept myself."

If this looks familiar, then that is because it is the basic foundation of the Emotional Freedom Technique tapping protocol, which would work equally well in place of this simplified exercise.

Exercise 3

Gratitude Journal

Whilst certainly not a novel idea, I am a great fan of keeping a gratitude journal. Taking a few minutes daily to acknowledge all that is positive in our lives can be very powerful soul medicine. It is especially helpful when life is making us "down."

I grew up with my Mum regularly reciting to me a poem about someone who complained that they had no shoes and who then met a man who had no feet. Frankly, it was lost on a small child and only irritated me, but after my flood, it was one of the first things that came to me and it helped a great deal. We can always choose to spin our life circumstances, but it is a deliberate choice. The choice is: I choose me.

A few final words of advice:

All of these exercises require a few minutes per day at least of commitment to your own life and healing journey. It's possible that you will experience levels of resistance to doing them. This is entirely normal, but growth and healing are achieved by regularly showing up in your own life. Just like any relationship, commitment and dedication is key. Without giving yourself time every day, nothing will change so: MAKE TIME, SHOW UP, DO THE WORK, PUT YOURSELF FIRST. You will be amazed at the results!

Blessings for your onward journey!

Debrah Goldston is a highly capable spiritual teacher with more than 30 years' experience in the mind, body, spirit arena.

A qualified solicitor and teacher, she is smart, business savvy and passionate about helping women to achieve their highest potential. Known for a tough talking approach that is underpinned with loving compassion, Debrah is capable of taking women to their "edge", where real shifts occur.

By blending a myriad of techniques, gathered through her extensive professional study of numerous healing modalities such as clinical hypnotherapy, NLP, numerology and psychology, together with her highly intuitive skills, Debrah leads her clients towards true empowerment and personal growth.

www.divine-feminine.co.uk

BANISH YOUR BLUES!

Grab a handy paintbrush,
Allow it to run rife!
Paint a vivid picture,
Penetrate your life.

A riot of rampant colour,
Redolent, raw and real,
Infiltrate inhibitions,
Reality reveal.

Wash away woeful worries,
Banish boring brown,
Obliterate with wild flurries,
Remnants of careworn frown.

Decorate possessions,
Daub as if possessed,
Splatter vivid colour,
Plaster over past regrets.

Relish rainbow revelations,
Brush away those blues!
Claim your inner artist,
Garnish with glowing, garish hues!

Sue Williams

Against All Odds

Debs de Vries

"I began with an idea and then it became something else".
— *Pablo Picasso.*

CLEARLY REMEMBER WONDERING if I was having a breakdown. I reflected that if this was true, the timing was really inconvenient. At that precise moment, I was standing in front of a room full of young lawyers and preparing to give them a day's training in problem solving and negotiation. I'd done it hundreds of times before. This was my professional life and up until that moment, I'd delivered this - and dozens of other programmes - with ease and enthusiasm. What was troubling me, as I looked at the faces in front of me, none of whom I knew? It was this; - I felt sure I'd seen each one of them before. I felt I knew their names, but I didn't. I had never worked in that company or even in that building. What was going on?

My belly churned as I tried to put these conflicting ideas together in my troubled mind. All I could do was to take a deep breath and launch into the programme, focusing solely on the moment. I soldiered on. It wasn't until the drive home that I could reflect in peace and get honest with myself.

The bald truth was, that for the last 12 months at least, I had felt I was getting 'stale' in my work. I'd done it too many times and even though I hadn't admitted it to myself before, my heart and mind were trying to tell me it was time to move on. I wasn't delivering from my passion anymore. It had become just 'a job'.

My earnest desire had always been to help people and I was good at it. As a child, I had felt the same way. As I looked at the small crowd of maybe 20 eager young lawyers in the room, I also suddenly knew I wanted to help millions, not dozens, of people. I was just scratching the surface of a huge need. Yet, I couldn't affect much change if I carried on offering what no longer fired me up. It would be an empty, false offering. In that moment I also knew I ached to be the coach and buddy by everyone's side, not just this small handful. How crazy an idea was that, in the year 1999, before the Internet changed the world?

Eventually, I stopped pretending things were fine and asked my (then) husband if I could step back from work for a while. We were comfortably provided for on his salary, we had a young son whom I just loved caring for, and he said 'yes'. I jumped in to the gap.

Within a week of leaving my practice, I found myself saying, "Yes" to a Reiki course. I really had no idea what Reiki was. Finding a spiritual outlet for my life was revelatory. Like a lot of people when they step into that flow, I became a 'spiritual junkie' – rooting out every course and teacher I could get my hands on.

My yoga practice went up a few notches: I began to meditate. While studying practical metaphysics, I realised I was lonely and unhappy in my marriage. I spoke to my husband about my desire to enjoy our relationship more: to be part of his social life and for him to enjoy and have fun with me. I hadn't expected him to turn his back on my request. He simply asserted he was happy with things just the way they were. He did not want to change.

Emotionally shattered at this unexpected turn of events, I threw myself deeper into my spiritual training. Then I had a dream, a dream of such power that I did not, could not, ignore its message. I signed up for a course in – Argentine Tango. In learning that most sultry, seductive and feminine of dances, I reignited my passion, my sexuality and even more amazingly my spiritual insight. I also developed a whopping crush on my dance teacher. Embarrassing, painful, exciting and scary. It was scary, as I did not want to risk my marriage on a crush.

I knew I had to 'fess up. I hoped this would be a turning point in the marriage: one in which we became closer and my husband woke up to my needs. But being honest with him about the crush, caused our marriage to falter and eventually die. It died slowly, coldly and without any real attempt to get to the underlying issues.

My solicitor later told me that men often plan to exit a marriage over a long term, preparing financially for the day. I wish I had known that before. It would have saved me trying to bend myself into a knot to get back into his good books. I would perhaps have sorted finances or organised a mutual exit plan.

I didn't, I just kept doing what I had always done. Keeping the peace. Getting smaller and weaker inside. Then I found a new male friend. This man lived in America. We met on line via my friend's site relating to spiritual matters. I was happy to have a male friend I could relate to. We talked about everything, mostly in daily emails. My ex found our emails and that was the last straw.

As he left the marriage, my perimenopause kicked in, as did all the buried fears of a lifetime. By the time I was 51 (two years later) I was broken; exhausted, living in a tiny rented house, trying to work and study, and making a reasonable mess of most things. I didn't want people to know how much of a state I was in and just how scared I was. I continued to bash onwards until my body shouted, "no more" and pinned me, weeping and helpless, into my bed.

I had to get well. It wasn't optional. So, I gave up my part time work and got state support. I went away on my own for a week and slept. When I came home, I saw that I had scrawled a couple of words on my desk jotter. The words were:

"voice artist".

As I stared at my handwriting, a huge shiver ran throughout my body. Voice artist? Yes, voice artist! That is what I had to do next. I was convinced, despite not having a clue what it entailed or how I could make it work. It was part of my destiny and I knew it.

So, let's fast-forward six months. I had had some proper training. I knew the basics of recording simple sound tracks and I had turned our spare bedroom into an amateur sound studio. What this meant was my late mother's room screen was doubling as a sound booth. I'd put foam against the bedroom windows, and it worked! I was proud of my resourcefulness. Back then, buying a sound booth for home was at least a £5k investment and a complete impossibility for me to finance.

I was doing auditions on line to get work. This helped me to learn my craft and I loved it, even though it pushed me way beyond my computer abilities at times. But I kept going and kept learning. Money was not showing up, but I didn't care too much at that stage. I was using my voice and it felt good.

Then, one ordinary weekday, as I went into the bedroom to record, a memory came back to me. I remembered how I had stood in that room full of lawyers and wished I could reach millions of people. That had happened five years ago – and in those five years the most amazing advances had happened in technology.

I got it in a flash. THIS was the answer to my prayer. I could reach out, via the Internet, and help millions of people to relax. With the innocence and faith of a child, I sat down and wrote a script with the idea that a radio station could broadcast to people who were driving, to help them chill. It was a simple as that.

After recording the script, I then hunted about on the Internet for a radio station to send it to. I didn't overthink; I just kept taking the next step. I found a station called "Chill" and I loved their ethic, so I sent the recording there. Then I pretty much forgot about it because I was due in court for the final hearing of our long running divorce and had a lot of paperwork to prepare.

A couple of weeks before the hearing I received an email from the station manager of "Chill". He, and his team in London ("they had a team in London?") loved my idea. Would I go into their local radio station and record some more? You bet I would! With a sense of pure joy, I wrote 10 more mini scripts and recorded them, leaving the radio station to do something called 'podcast' them. At that point, I was completely focused on the divorce and forgot about this thing called 'podcasting'. I was just deliriously happy to have put my idea into the world.

The judge found in my favour. I came home with a huge burden lifted from my shoulders and a sense of new beginnings. There was a message on my answer phone.

It was Bern, the station manager from "Chill". I slid slowly onto the floor as he spoke:

"Debs, your podcast has become the World's Number one download in iTunes and in the American health charts. If it had downloaded 2,000 times, we'd have been well pleased. If it had hit 10,000, we would have been stunned. However, it has exceeded that figure and way beyond – 30,000 and counting. We have no idea why. But there it is."

Flowers, champagne and newspaper reporters arrived the next day. But nothing came close to hearing Bern tell me that my desire, my need to reach out and help, had come to life and had made an impact across the globe.

Here are three things that I would really recommend you focus on during change or times of crisis.

1. Even though no one else can see or feel what is in your heart, you can. If it feels true to you, even when it defies 'common sense', even when other people tell you it's ridiculous, you are the keeper of this knowledge. Write it down, draw it, dance it, talk about it - find a way to make it real in small ways. Make space for it in your life, no matter how small that space, and nurture it.

2. Be super kind to yourself. Nurture your body and your mind. Find ways to let go of things that drain you and do not share dreams or ideas with people who will doubt you. Protect your dreams and find like-minded people who will support you and cheer you on.

3. Joseph Campbell said; "If you can see the path ahead, it's not your path. Your path is the one you make . . ." You are going into uncharted territory as soon as you step off the beaten track you've been used to. You can expect that to feel scary but inside of you is strength far greater than you can imagine right now. Even if, as you read this, you doubt me, I can assure you it's as true for you as it was for me. I'm not special, not different, just bigger and stronger than I knew. It was my dream that helped me be this woman. Just

as your dreams are there to help you grow, no matter what your age, your abilities or your finances.

Debs de Vries offers women a unique path of growth in their perimeno-pausal stage of life. By addressing all four areas of life - physical, emotional, psychological and spiritual (not just physical symptoms) Debs helps women uncover and access the hidden power that is their birthright.

Debs uses tools that she has developed in 30 years of teaching, training and healing. She's a Transference Healer™ Reiki Master, Yoga teacher, professional mentor, and coach. Her Menopause EVEolution method helps women and their families to live more fulfilled and magical lives as do her books and articles. Find out more at www. debsdevries.com

HE DIED

My man died
Broke my heart
Broke my life

There is silence now
Where once there was noise
Sweet words of love, were they?

Despair challenges the mind
Was it simply this?
The habit of being two

Not true my heart rebels
Sweet words enriched our lives
Gave us certainty and hope

Oh, that once again
Our hearts would leap with joy
For that happy noise we shared

Elizabeth Beetham

Surviving and Living

Elizabeth Beetham

I MISS MY MAN.

I remember my 50th Birthday as if it was yesterday. It was truly a wonderful celebration. My darling husband John made it perfect, as my life was at that time. In fact, I used to say, "I have the perfect life!" When he died suddenly and dramatically in a car park in Totnes, leaving without being able to say goodbye; my life was shattered. It was devastating.

Our society is adept at discussing every subject possible from politics to all the obscure forms of sexual gratification but when it comes to death, loss, and the resulting grief we are like ostriches burying our heads in the sand, not wanting these things to touch our lives.

Death is our constant companion. Although we resist this thought it is the only certainty in life, we all die. Sorry to remind you but it is true and as someone told me many years ago "Death is such a final thing." When I heard that I thought what a silly thing to say but it is worth considering. Imagine how much more fulfilling our lives would be if we could embrace this concept, even if only some of the time. I do urge you to do so, never forget to tell your loved ones how much you love them and how much you care. You may lose the opportunity as I did and then regret it very much indeed.

There are various stages of grieving which you go through slowly and painfully. One of them is certainly regret; why didn't I realise he was so ill. Why didn't I go with him to see the consultant and the main one for me - why didn't I love him more? Why didn't I appreciate all the small things he did for me and show appreciation? It is a constant habit and a very human trait that we quickly take our loved ones for granted. In all relationships this trait is often the reason for arguments and resentment.

Anger is another stage where you hate the world, you hate yourself and you also hate the person you loved for leaving you alone. Why did he have to go and why are you so alone not able to function as you once did? You feel lost and isolated, everything about your life changed in the instant that your loved one died. You look for comfort, but my experience was that the gulf was so enormous that I did feel totally lost; like being out in the middle of the ocean, all alone, in a small rowing boat with no oars.

Grief is sometimes overwhelming. It takes you by surprise and envelops your life like a wicked black cloud hanging just above your head. The sense of loss, a physical pain which crying does not relieve; your heart does truly ache which sounds unbelievable, but I can assure you it is true. You ask, "Where is he? Is he ok? Does he know how much I loved him?" Useless thoughts and memories fill your days, but you do go on because you know he would want you to; I did and still feel I go on for both of us. Grief is very personal. It is an uncharted journey which as I want to remind you, we all must travel at some time.

I wrote the following which gives you a flavour of my feelings and I think is also hopefully a little amusing.

Ashes to Ashes

When John died the shock was terrible. One moment he was there beside me in the car, and then as I was trying to manoeuvre, he got out to try and find a parking space. Another car moved out a little behind, and while I was concentrating on parking, John had a massive heart attack. Suddenly, within a few minutes he was gone. Why was he so angry about a silly car parking space? Why did I not rush from the car to stop him? The bereaved are always left with unanswered questions and of course those regrets.

The days that followed seemed so unreal. Could he survive this massive heart attack? But I knew in my heart that he was gone. He stopped breathing at the car park and then twice in the ambulance. There was really no hope. But you do hope, while there is life there is always hope. He looked so strange hooked up to those awful machines. When the Consultant told us that they felt it best to turn off the ventilator, it just seemed inevitable. My John was gone. I would not hear his voice again or see those green smiling eyes. His body, just the remaining shell of my wonderful husband - was a strong body. It took a few days. Horrible painful exhausting days, waiting for that last breath.

Then the drive home without him, and the days after, when I lived like an automaton. Thank God the children took over and sorted out the funeral. I knew he wanted to be cremated but he would have hated all the fuss. A quiet funeral would have been best, but you get swept up in 'Doing the right thing!'

The day arrived and it was hideous. With strength from above and determination, I kept my dignity despite the purgatory of the day.

I thought of his ashes languishing at the undertakers. It was playing on my mind. I even dreamed that all the red plastic jars, neatly labelled at the undertakers talked to each other at night. They were bobbing about trying to fall off the shelves, trying to escape. They moaned and asked each other when so and so would get off their fat ass and come and get me! I woke feeling guilty. I must collect him and take him where I felt he could rest in peace.

The family and I had discussed where John's ashes should go while we were at the hospital. His children wanted to be involved but I was strong now and able to voice my true feelings. They had their own way about the funeral, this final journey was just for him and me.

John was an adventurer, a mountaineer; he had climbed Aconcagua in Argentina the year we met, at 22,837ft it was an amazing achievement. He loved nothing more than being on some high summit and he loved the Lake District. He holidayed there as a child and we had spent many happy times there fell walking together.

It took all my strength to collect him and sign the paper to release his ashes from that cold and clinical place. Once I had put the large red plastic jar in the car I felt better. It was much heavier than I had thought it would be. I was worried I would not be able to carry him up the mountain, but we were on our way. I talked to him and cried on that final journey up to our favourite hotel, in the Lake District.

When you are alone simple things become more difficult. You worry about things that in the past you would not have even considered. I was afraid I would burst into tears as soon as I saw a familiar face. Jessica, my guide for the walk, met me and helped me with my things. I carried John to the room. "It is ok. Everything will be fine" I kept telling myself.

The weather was perfect for the walk and I carried my dear man on my back up to a high summit of 1090 meters. Typically for me, I did not like the first place as there were no views of the lakes, but I soon found the perfect spot with views of Windermere, and Grasmere. It was sad of course but I felt proud and happy when I left him on the hillside. It is aptly called Great Rig, near Fairfield Horseshoe summit. Who knows, life is full of mysteries, but I am sure I felt his presence and his gratitude. I can think of him now walking those hills and being happy. It was a fitting tribute to my man. I will be eternally grateful for our life together.

What I now understand and have considered a lot is that grief is not just about losing a loved one. Grief is a part of all of our lives and comes in many difference guises. I hope that these words will help you to realise this and think of it not as the enemy but something to accept.

Most women in their 50s are experiencing or have experienced the menopause, a change of life as it is often called. As a nutritionist I can assure you that the menopause is not an illness but a natural part of a woman's life, but it can be a very difficult and a frightening time. In particular hot flushes can be so debilitating and exhausting. There can also be a sense of loss and many women suffer grief at this time which I certainly did. It can be because they have never had a child, or it can be because they would have liked more children or even the realisation that the choice has been taken from them, which can bring on the feelings of loss and grief.

I had both my children at a young age. I never felt that I had planned a new arrival or indeed enjoyed the feeling of excitement and anticipation which many women have when they are pregnant. Although of course they were both loved and cherished as babies and indeed even more now, neither were planned and I felt I had missed out on something joyful.

As part of my work as a Natural Health Consultant I hope that I have helped many women express and realise that women do experience these feelings of loss and grief, they are normal and nothing to regret or feel ashamed about. I want you to know that the menopause is not the end but a wonderful and magical beginning to the next stage of your life.

As women over 50 become more visible and vocal we must applaud and enjoy their success and believe in our own. I believe that the post menopause stage is a wonderful time of freedom and development; you are more confident now so let this shine from you. Make this stage of your life the very best so that you can embrace old age with a sense of fulfilment and grace. For me this has certainly been the case and although I felt desolate when I lost my husband what I now know is life is for the living.

I hope the rest of my life will be a credit to him because he gave me so much and still does. I feel and sense his strength has carried me through the desperate times and I have achieved many successes since his death. This success has been with the help and support of wonderful friends and family, for which I am eternally grateful. Take pleasure in living it's a wonderful gift, given freely.

Exercises

1. What helped me enormously the first two years after John died was yoga. I cannot recommend yoga enough. It is a fantastic way of relaxing the body and mind, while giving you flexibility and strength. Try this simple yogic breathing exercise whenever you are feeling stressed. Sit comfortably and take a deep breath with your mouth closed and your tongue gently touching the roof of your

mouth near your teeth. Now breathe out slowly, parting your lips very slightly while relaxing your tongue on the bottom of your mouth. Continue this form of breathing for a few minutes. It is a very subtle and effective way of calming the body and mind.

2. Do not isolate yourself even though you may want to run away and be alone. Please avoid doing this, because if you are grieving you need to keep busy and to be with other people with who you will find comfort. I joined a "Singing for Fun" group and it has been amazing and fulfilling. I have learned to appreciate music more; made new friends and laughed a lot. Before each session we have to warm up our vocal cords. Try this, it is fun – pretend you have a paper plane between your fingers and thumb and blow it across the room. You expel all that stale air and fill your lungs with fresh well oxygenated air which provides your body with more energy.

3. I have found writing poetry a profound and cathartic way of expressing my feelings. Poetry does not have to rhyme, just put pen to paper and write. It can be just for your own eyes only or eventually as I have you can publish your work. I published "Life Love Loss" which you can find on Amazon. It was a fantastic feeling to see my book in print. Many of the love poems were written for John as of course were the loss poems but it tells the journey through my life and it is now out there for all to read. I hope it will bring comfort to some. They say poetry is the out- pouring of the soul so why not try and write a poem today? You may be very surprised at what you can achieve; after all you only have to Believe!

Live with joy and Health.

Elizabeth Beetham is a professional health journalist, broadcaster, nutritionist and wellbeing expert who writes regularly for a range of UK periodicals and a New York newspaper. A former company director and management consultant, she made a radical career change 15 years ago to gain a BSc in Holistic Nutrition and founded her company Power for Health in 2004. She empowers and motivates her clients to embrace a healthier lifestyle, and has led workshops for clients such as Morgan Stanley in New York and National Grid in the UK.

A regular guest on BBC local radio speaking on health topics, she is also an experienced public speaker. Her Healthy Living for Life Program has proved successful in changing many clients' lives. Elizabeth is passionate about inspiring others, particularly business leaders, to lead a healthier life. www.powerforhealth.com

RIGHT TO WRITE

Don't despair,
It's all in there,
Inside of you;
The truth of who you are.
You have travelled far on your journey.

Depressed yourself? Express yourself!
Reassess yourself; address yourself:
"What lessons have I learned?"
What has been churned up,
Burned up?

How have you earned
The right to write?
By having a hand, a pen,
The yen to begin.
When if not now?

How? Wow, however you like!
Psych yourself up, roll up your sleeves.
No-one grieves she who leaves in silence,
Too weak to speak her truth.

Youth yearns to live; you have wisdom
To give; insight, meaning.
Defined your learning,
Created meaning; gleaning
Nuances, where once there were none.

Battles fought; a war of words ensues,
Flashing swords; regalia.
Banish feelings of failure;
Nail your colours to the mast,

You've had a blast,
Explode on to the page!

Be a sage. You've earned
It; spurned it
Time after time,
When more pressing matters
Or words of flatterers
Carried weight. Abate
The doubters; flouters
Of convention gather.

Work up a lather, create a palaver.
Speak your truth, for you embody
Both wisdom and youth.
Splatter the page with grey matter,
Cause a clatter of appreciation,
A hushed intake of breath.
Scared to death, or scared of death?

Whilst you have breath, keep on breathing
Life into the world.
Talents unfurl, a whirl of wit and wonder.
No longer chunder; how could you bore?
Thunder and lightning embrace.

Shake up complacency,
You've earned seniority,
Leave a legacy
Not just plain white space.

Sue Williams

The Impact of Approaching Fifty

Elizabeth Gordon

*"Success is a journey, not a destination. The doing is often
more important than the outcome."*
— *Arthur Ashe*

A T THE AGE of 38, I experienced the crash of burnout and was subsequently diagnosed with ME/Chronic Fatigue Syndrome. My journey back to good health involved a very long process of mostly trial and error. At times, I had managed to reach a point of feeling back to my former levels of health, only to slide back with some unexpected problem. I had continued to take care of my health basics like nutrition, water, and sleep.

Despite always loving exercise, it seemed to create more health problems than benefits. My natural competitive streak would emerge, and I always liked to challenge myself to do more and more. I enjoyed being out in nature and walking and running. At some points, I would manage to achieve goals of doing a 5km run, then a 10km run using a run/walk approach, but I couldn't seem to manage to sustain my health consistently.

As I approached 50, the voices in my head grew ever stronger. I was adamant that I wasn't happy with a half-life existence and feeling constrained in my actions. My three children were moving rapidly towards adulthood, and two were at university. My eldest son had already been on several travel adventures including a World Challenge to Africa and a trek to Everest Base Camp, that were completely beyond any of my experiences. I dreamed of being completely well and able to do purposeful work to support other women to achieve better self-care and business success and to go off on amazing travel adventures.

So, one day, I was reading a fitness magazine and saw an advert for a charity trek to Everest Base Camp – powerful impulses took over and compelled me to sign up without really considering the practicalities. Everest was somewhere that had always fascinated me, and seeing my son's photos and hearing of his amazing experiences had brought it back to the forefront of my mind. Being able to actually see and experience the highest mountain in the world seemed symbolic of reaching my full life potential and taking empowered action.

The trek was due to take place almost two years ahead, and I believed that would give me time to really focus on extending the boundaries of my health and fitness, and raise the requisite funds for the worthwhile charity. My husband thought I was crazy and worried about me, while the children were encouraging me to go for it!

First, I started walking longer and longer distances on the canals near my home. Then my eldest son and I went to Snowdon (the highest mountain in Wales) to give me some experience of walking and climbing with ascents and descents. It was really hard going to keep up with a fit young man in his early twenties on a sunny day. I was determined to keep pace, and he probably didn't fully understand my levels of health.

Instead of an easy route, he had taken us up one of the most difficult ascents via a challenging rocky ridge with mostly sheer drops on either side. As I got more tired, a group came in the opposite direction; my concentration wavered, then I fell in what seemed one of those slow-motion sequences, imagining either a major injury or the end of me… Fortunately, the universe was in a kind mood that day, and my anticipated long fall was actually halted by some rocks on the left side below the ridge. Yet, if I'd fallen the other way, things would probably have been very different.

I felt very shocked at first, then gradually realised that I had bad gashes and severe bruising to one knee, but I was relatively okay. Although the crazy side of me still hoped to reach the top, it was obvious that we had to stop and try to return down the mountain to our start point. This took over three hours of agony with every step, but I was alive!

For some reason, we didn't even think of trying to get help to get off the mountain. The following week, I saw on the news that someone else had fallen in a similar spot but was rescued by a helicopter flown by a British prince - a missed opportunity for a spectacular rescue!

As you can imagine, this incident put me off doing exercise for some time, but I still just saw it as an unfortunate accident rather than a sign I was doing too much. I went back to my long canal walks eventually, and continued to believe in my dream.

However, the fund-raising then started to feel quite stressful as I worried about letting down those who supported me if my health didn't progress as I'd hoped. I continued to try to push myself onwards until one day I collapsed while out shopping. I didn't recover as expected, so I was taken by the ambulance to a nearby hospital, with extremely low blood pressure that took many hours to return to normal. It took this second warning from my body to make me fully realise the risks of going on a remote trek at high altitudes to prove to myself that I could be well again. This experience would have potentially had a very different outcome in a remote environment. I couldn't put myself or my family through that level of worry and stress, so I reluctantly accepted the need to cancel and look for less extreme approaches.

Both experiences had caused my life to flash before my eyes and recognise that I had much more life left to live fully, memories to create with my family, and had bigger work left to do.

Finally, I realised that my mindset was the key area that I needed to focus on, together with implementing sustainable levels of exercise. I was naturally a driven, determined person, so learning to always be within my limits was extremely difficult and frustrating.

Slowly, the penny dropped, and I saw that small actions each day could still create progress. I came across an online thirty-day walking for thirty minutes challenge and created my own version. I felt that being able to walk every day meant that I wasn't ill, and I felt the embodied success of doing this consistently for thirty days, then sixty and ninety days. This was a continuous thread that I didn't want to allow to break if possible. But I still had those old patterns of behaviour and thoughts that were hard to change, so my walks soon grew to sixty minutes and longer.

My success started me thinking of bigger goals like a long-distance walk. I had seen images of the London Moonwalk and my daughter was enthusiastic about doing it together. I knew many women who had experienced breast cancer, so the fundraising element was important.

I trained very thoroughly by increasing my distances for a long walk each week to get as ready as possible for coping with over twenty-six miles. But I couldn't prepare for the overnight timings as the event is run at night and takes over eight hours of walking around central London.

At the time, I coped better than my daughter who had the confidence of her youth to do absolutely no preparation, but I took much longer to recover afterwards, although, there were no major health problems at last. So, the very simple act of walking outdoors every day was another key health breakthrough. It was the consistent daily action that created the positive shifts, not my extreme challenges that created mini-crashes and potentially undid the benefits.

Heading towards 50 also made me feel I sometimes needed to be more sensible, without losing that naturally impulsive and rebellious side. Setting goals that were realistic and achievable and not just dreaming was another aspect I struggled with. I'm naturally full of ideas and possibilities and often have a butterfly-like attention span when it comes to completing and finishing a project.

Like many people, I also often succumbed to "shiny object syndrome" and found myself investing in things that promised to transform my health or my business. Somehow, they generally didn't work for me as I struggled to devote time and energy, or found myself needing yet more things to make the first thing happen, or they were just a blueprint that didn't fit my life. It seemed like a constant quest for an elusive holy grail.

My experiences described in this story show that being overambitious may sometimes prove hazardous, particularly for those with a health condition impacting energy levels. Even when working with a coach, it's still possible to keep health issues hidden, find yourself agreeing to actions when you know that you're already fully committed, and then feeling a failure or avoiding the next session when you haven't made the desired progress. There had to be a way of being more consistently objective for people like me!

My awareness about developing health and exercise was in many ways considerably ahead of developing business strategies that worked for my health, but I started to see some transferable techniques. A key one was to set small actions that you felt were 100% achievable without creating energy problems - always keeping within your capacity rather than trying to exceed it.

Over time, I realised that there was actually more progression as this avoided having to negotiate the long pauses of injury or exhaustion, followed by the climb back to recovery and starting again. The consistency of action and developing new long-term habits have actually been one of the most effective sources of achieving change. Regular journaling and reviewing also help me to notice the impact of the small steps I am taking.

Three Exercises on Reality Checking

1. Stop and explore your goal in more detail. I like to use the SMARTERS approach. More research may be needed to fill in any gaps.

   - Specific - can you include more detail and clarity on your desired outcomes?

   - Measurable - a mix of quantity (e.g. time, money) and quality (how your life would be different).

- Achievable - do you have access to the external resources you need (e.g. financial, equipment, training).

- Realistic - do you have the internal resources such as sufficient time, commitment, and determination to overcome what might get in your way? If you have a health condition, always aim to stay well within your current level of capability.

- Time-bound - is there a clear start and end date, with interim milestones?

- Enthusiasm - do you have the energy and passion to make this happen? If you would give yourself a score of below 9 out of 10, how could you increase this?

- Recorded - writing down the goal, planning the steps and reviewing progress.

- Supported - access to the necessary support and accountability you may need on your journey.

2. Share your plans with someone you know and trust, but who will also have the ability to offer you a combination of high support and high challenge to allow you to learn and develop on your journey. They can provide honest feedback and challenge you to do better and offer a different perspective. This may be a coach or an accountability buddy for example.

3. Review and adapt – When you start your journey, there may be lots of aspects where you don't know what you don't know. Gradually, you start to become aware of these and move towards being competent, but it still requires a lot of effort, so be prepared to go through these phases. Eventually, it can become an unconscious easy habit. Learning to drive a car is an example we can probably all relate to.

4. Depending on the size of your goal, I would recommend breaking them down into interim 90-day goals, and then monthly and weekly sub-goals and action steps. Review what's working and what you need to change or adapt. As part of this, I would encourage you to always focus on your current results and notice and celebrate the

improvement, NOT compare them to some ideal results. This will create a positive cycle of encouraging self-talk, more motivation and confidence, and prompt more actions towards the goal.

Elizabeth Gordon is passionate about supporting women in business to be healthy, aligned with their desired lifestyle and purpose, and working towards financial freedom and business success. She believes that health and energy are the foundation, followed by mindset, and then focus on business improvement.

After a career in accountancy, Elizabeth initially started her own professional accountancy practice to create a better fit with family and personal values, until life events led to burnout and a diagnosis of ME/ Chronic Fatigue Syndrome. Elizabeth developed coaching skills during a long recovery journey, and a passion for supporting other women to recognise the importance of wellbeing and self-care to their success. She is proud to be part of The Chrysalis Effect to support the recovery of those diagnosed with ME, Chronic Fatigue and Fibromyalgia.

Elizabeth is married to Tim, and they have three wonderful adult children. She loves being outdoors in nature, walking and other forms of exercise, photography and exploring new places.

For further information, please visit www.femalesuccess.com

NEW LIGHT

Opening my heart
To a brand-new vision of Life
I found you
FINALLY!
And
You were in my eyes all along,
Although I fought hard
To stay blinkered
You
Who coaxed me across the threshold,
And down a darkened tumbling path.
You
Who shone your light
On the many shoots still thriving
Amid blustering jagged rocks
And
You who prised my eyes wide open
To the magical journey called Life!
You.
You were in my eyes all along.
You

Gillian Holland

Connections to Spirit

Gillian Holland

"Being your own Medium and letting your heart rule your head." Gillian Holland

I F YOU'D TOLD me as a kid, that when I grew up, I would be working as a medium in sometimes packed spiritualist churches giving messages of hope and inspiration to people who'd lost their loved ones, I would never have believed you. All that spirit stuff, well it's kinda 'woo-woo', isn't it? But an experience at an ordinary yoga class which I felt drawn to attend, was to change the way I understood life as well as death and my understanding of mediumship.

An encounter with my much-loved mum after she died, set me off on quite a journey, which to date has spanned over 40 years. As I was to learn, there's a lot more to life...and death than meets the eye.

Until mum died, when I was just 25 years, I was thoroughly enjoying life as a primary school teacher. All my thoughts were directed towards progressing my career, and although I had an interest in things esoteric, I'd embarked on my Open University Psychology Honours Degree with my career in mind. Little did I realise at the time that my degree, the Masters which followed, and my existing teaching qualification were to come in very handy in my new role as a medium. The Spirit World had other plans for me.

I was determined to get to that yoga class come what may, even though I was still wrapped in grief. I'd been fascinated by yoga for quite some time, even half-heartedly thought about having a go, but the feeling this time was quite different: I just had to get there. No excuses!

Classes, in those days were all about postures rather than meditation and relaxation. This one, however, included all three aspects and therefore really intrigued me.

Once at the class I had no problem floating off into a blissful state of relaxation as the meditation began. Stretched out on the floor and wrapped securely under my blanket, I sighed and breathed a very long breath out, letting go of some of my pent-up emotions. It felt as if I was sinking into infinite bliss.

The light on my inner screen was just a tiny blip to begin with, but it rapidly grew into a brilliance. There was something about it, which seemed increasingly familiar, although I couldn't quite put my finger on it. I sighed once more as the light began to morph into form...mum! And my world lit up once again!

Mum was standing in the middle of a bridge of light, smiling straight back at me, arms outstretched looking radiant, happy and peaceful beyond words. This was the mum of old, apparently back in the pink of health, nothing like the shell I'd seen collapsed on the kitchen floor a few weeks beforehand.

The love emanating from her was phenomenal; it had a purity I'd never experienced before. What a gift that was, especially when I look back on it all those years ago. This experience proved to be the basis of all my future spiritual understanding. Spiritualism is a philosophy. It has a lot to tell us about 'the continuity of life.' We, along with the rest of the natural world, are continually changing form. A butterfly evolves, for instance, from caterpillar, and cocoon before it ultimately transforms into a butterfly. As human beings we merely release our physical bodies but the rest of us lives on in the after-life. We continue to learn throughout our life-time, and beyond. Acting on our intuition is a part of the adventure.

In my 50's, 60's and now freshly into my seventh decade, I continue to learn. Listening to my gut instinct has led me to some really powerful experiences, one in an ancient Mayan temple in Mexico. It also pushed me into studying my family tree, 'before it was too late,' which led me to find my 90-year-old uncle, and a host of cousins I didn't even know existed. Each experience really transformed my life again.

Hitting your fiftieth year, and each new decade after that, is always a milestone. The inevitable ageing process can be quite hard to bear, and I feel sometimes we can just opt for cosy security. Understanding our lives here on earth, are a part of a much bigger picture has not only helped me come to terms with my own mortality, but to remain open to the adventure of life. What's more, age isn't a barrier on your journey of self-discovery.

Mum certainly didn't want to see me grieving for the rest of my life, neither would my dad, who passed over to the other side when I was just four and a half. They inspired me from spirit to go out there and have a go, as I know all our departed loved ones would want us to do. I had a whale of a time exploring Switzerland by myself when I hit 70. Later this year I'm off again to Australia, visiting the places I missed last time, and then of course there's the book to write. It's never too late to have an adventure. My good friend published her first book in her 80's!

Although you may be more familiar with what is known as evidential mediumship, the kind of thing you see in spiritualist churches or even on TV, I believe intuition is a far more powerful way of communicating with the other side of life, because it transforms your thinking process, too. We just have to listen to our intuition.

Evidential mediumship may satisfy the intellect, but intuition works directly with your heart, rather than your mind, and this connection aligns you with your Soul's Purpose. Your intellect equips you for life here on earth, whereas your intuition relates to your progress as an Eternal Being. We on earth need to balance our earthly survival needs with our soul's need to expand and grow. So, intuition is designed to take you to another level altogether. It helps you take a more detached look at something your head can't get itself round.

Equally I'm sure you may also have your own amazing experiences to share. So, don't allow your intellect to undervalue or even dismiss them either. As a more mature person, you not only have intuition on your side, but a wealth of experience too. The good news is you don't have to be a medium in the conventional sense to receive a communication from Spirit: you just have to open your mind. Write any experience down in a journal and allow the experience to expand your thinking. Dare to share them too. You'll find you are not alone. You do have something to say, we all do. People are waking up to the power of Spirit, and you are a part of that mighty wave.

Honouring our feelings isn't always easy because over the centuries we've been taught to dismiss them, in favour of the intellect or reasoning power. Your intellect will try everything in its power to stop you following your passion. It will tell you, it's too late, you're not up to the mark, even, who do you think you are? Your life, though is not meant to be powered by struggle and conflict, it's meant to be powered by love.

Remember intuition is your own inbuilt connection to Spirit and your Soul's Purpose and nobody else's; you don't need any specialist long term training, because it's an inherent part of your innate wisdom.

The good news is that most of us are already familiar with gut instincts. We just need to sharpen our skills up a bit, give our internal GPS the attention it deserves.

Intuition serves us on a day to day basis, too. It invites you to approach each new day as if it's your first…and last here on earth. You might know it, as I do, as an irresistible urge to get out into the open countryside when life hems you in, or to take in that Oscar winning movie, or just switch on some music to dance, dance, dance! It's designed to take you out of the ordinary into the extraordinary, and is the perfect anecdote for all your pent- up emotions. Taking time out for any one of those activities may just give you the inspiration you're looking for to take the next evolutionary step forward. That's what happened to me.

When times get tough, we revert to automatic pilot to carry us through the day. This creates a hard, protective shell, and we lose heart. Although it's meant to protect, it can completely cut us off from our feelings and emotions and life. Honouring your intuition is an essential act of self -love, and it's this light which gives us the inspiration to carry on when the going gets tough. I was completely stuck in my self-imposed cocoon until my encounter with mum. I'm just so grateful I chose to follow my instincts that day.

Our intuition is a bright star of hope which carries us through the dark times into fresh fields. When we honour our intuition, it takes us into previously uncharted waters. These inspirations can be the starting point for another exciting journey, no matter your age.

Every day our intuition walks by our side, and so do our spirit friends. We are all born to sparkle, so sticking to a strict but very secure routine, just dulls the light you were born to share. Love really does makes the world go around. Befriend your intuition. It is the light which brings hope back into your world. It certainly brought hope back into mine.

Gillian's three tips

1. Befriend and learn to trust your intuition. It's on your side and may be felt as a sensation or feeling from out of the blue. It's designed to take you on an adventure into a new brighter reality. Adopt a balanced approach. Intuitions aren't intended to lead you into danger, but designed to take you on an adventure into a new brighter reality.

2. If you are drawn to, create space in your diary to spend time out in nature. Then keep a journal. Spending time out in nature connects you to your Soul's Purpose. I connect quite naturally to the Spirit World out of doors. It's so relaxing. I find my memory soars, then connects me to a memory which in its turn connects me to a loved one.

3. Intuition is generally quite spontaneous. It happens when you least expect it. Don't try too hard. The last thing I expected on that day was an encounter with mum. Stay as open as you possibly can, prepare to be amazed. It's designed to bring sparkle back into your life.

Gillian Holland is a medium of over thirty years standing. She has worked out in Spain on a regular basis, and also France together with the USA. She not only works from her home in Hertfordshire offering one to one sessions, but in local churches and centres too. Gillian offers regular angel meditation classes and spiritual awareness groups, and is currently completing a book. Her interest in psychology has helped in her chosen career. She believes Spirit communicates with us in a variety of ways including the conventional 'evidential' mediumship we see on TV. Although this satisfies our intellect; our Intuition which truly opens our heart to life's magic, and can also connect us to our Soul's Purpose. Lightupyourspirit.blogspot.co.uk

RAY OF HOPE

Move ever closer to the Rapture
Sweet Sister of Light.
Be Still
Hold no fear
Let it enfold
And then move you
Fill you up with unbounded waves of deep delight.
As you surrender to its ancient rhythms
Remembering
That you are indeed pure Light.
And the veil that so enthralled you
Rendering you blind
And unable to see?
Ah
That's the illusion,
It stopped you breathing
……And moving
O now you are free
Come dance now
Celebrate
And in the light of this reawakening world,
Remember
In the Silence
As I move you
I
AM
YOUR DESTINY

Gillian Holland

Life Begins at Fifty

Helen Carver

"Twenty years from now, you will be more disappointed
by the things that you didn't do than by the ones you did.
So, throw off the bowlines. Sail away from the safe harbour.
Catch the trade winds in your sails.
Explore. Dream. Discover."
— *Mark Twain*

AT THE AGE of 49, having recently divorced after years of separation, I was both physically and mentally at rock bottom. Having 'waded through treacle' for the previous three years, I was desperately looking for some light at the end of the tunnel and thinking that there must be more to life than my present situation. As usual, in times of stress, I picked up a motivational book, and this one told me I could have whatever I wanted in life. Hmm! But, as I turned the last page, I asked myself, 'Okay, Helen, if you *could* have anything you wanted, what would you really want?' The answer that pinged back to me was as clear as a bell - to travel the world. Yeah, right! How could a mere mortal like me jack in her job and go off without a care?

Before I'd thought of the consequences, I asked my youngest daughter, Rachel, if she fancied travelling with me.

'Ooh, yes! That would be brilliant, Mum! Brilliant! Ooh, when are we going? Wahoo!'

Ooh, err, hang on a minute, I mean I wasn't serious, it was just a thought, and, err...oh noooo! Another fine mess I'd got myself into... or was it? You see, the logical, practical me was saying, 'What about my job, my mortgage, my security, my relationship?' But the crazy, wild, adventurous me was saying, 'It will be phenomenal, life-changing, ecstatic, liberating, wonderful.' Guess which one won?

Within four months, I'd left my long-standing job in our independent estate agency, rented my house out and planned the trip of a lifetime with my 19-year-old daughter in tow. My eldest daughter, Nicola, was spending five months in Mexico as part of her language degree, so it seemed like perfect timing. It was now or never, really. It was both exciting and terrifying in equal measure, but after a friend said, 'Helen, we don't want to be having a conversation in ten years' time with me saying to you, "Do you remember when you had that fantastic opportunity to travel the world?", it became a no-brainer. I didn't want to regret *not* going for the rest of my life.

So, two weeks after my 50th birthday, we set off on our world trip, which incorporated South Africa, Mexico, San Francisco, Hawaii, Maui, Fiji, New Zealand, Australia, Borneo, Singapore, Malaysia, Thailand, Hong Kong, China and, finally, Sri Lanka. To say that our trip was life-changing is an absolute understatement. It was mind-blowingly brilliant!

We experienced different foods and cultures, met wild and wonderful characters (many of whom are now life-long friends) and tried some seriously crazy antics, mainly in New Zealand, the adventure capital of the world. We went white-water rafting over a 7-metre waterfall, skydiving at 15,000 feet, hiked up a glacier, jumped off a waterfall and even posed naked in front of one (how could I refuse?). Once you've accomplished one daredevil sport, you suddenly feel invincible, as if you've won an Olympic gold medal and realise that you're capable of so much more than you ever thought possible. In fact, one guy on the Kiwi Experience Coach taking us around North and South Island gave me the best compliment ever.

'Helen, we don't think of you as Rachel's mum; you're just one of the gang.'

How lovely was that? But, then, I suppose I wasn't just a spectator waving them off as they did those madcap things; I was out there living it with them. A friend's son commented on Facebook, 'You two are some crazy bitches', which I took as rather a compliment. To be called a crazy bitch at 50 is, after all, quite an achievement!

You see, travelling gives you a completely different perspective on life. You realise that the people you meet along the way are not interested in age, creed or religion. As a fellow traveller, you are open to conversation, friendship and laughing, and seem genuinely immune to the mundane whines and woes of everyday life; probably because every day is really an adventure.

You're never quite sure who you're going to meet, where you're going to end up or what you're going to come across, and that can be scary, but also unbelievably exciting and liberating. It makes you feel *alive* because you're really *living* rather than just *existing*! And isn't that why we were put on this earth? To be happy, joyous, wild, crazy; to experience new things, go with the flow, talk to strangers, make new friends and be the best we can be? Of course, it is. It's just that sometimes we forget because we get immersed in the cocoon of our so-called comfortable lives.

Inevitably, we also had our fair share of scrapes and misadventures on our travels, too. I started driving on the wrong side of the road when turning right at a spaghetti junction in New Zealand and suddenly, three lanes of traffic were heading straight towards us. We couldn't get cash out of any cash points in Sri Lanka, and I had no more credit cards left. We didn't have an Indian Visa, so we had to stay in the holding lounge at Bombay Airport for hours as if we were illegal immigrants.

However, when we did end up in a tricky situation, I just tried to clear my mind, decide, and have faith that everything would turn out alright. And it usually did, because by coping with one problem, you learn to cope with the next. And after a while, you realise that you can deal with almost any situation. And the magical moments more than made up for the challenges: watching turtles hatch their eggs on a beach in Borneo, breath-taking sunsets in Mexico, living on paradise islands in Fiji, camping out on Frazer Island in Australia, riding on elephants in Thailand, and seeing the Terracotta Warriors in China. Ooh, I could go on and on.

Obviously, one of the biggest challenges about going away was wondering what on earth I was going to do when I got back. After two weeks of euphoria, telling all and sundry about our trip (with Rachel rolling her eyes as if to say, 'Oh no, not this tale again!'), I decided to write a book. I'd always said I was going to write a book and now, I thought, I'm damn well going to do it.

I'd kept a diary whilst we were away, and thus, *Life Begins at Fifty* was born, a humorous account of our trip. The best advice I was given was to just 'bash it out', otherwise, I'd never have got past the first page as I'd have been editing and re-editing it to perfection. My sister, very helpfully, gave me a 'Comprehensive Writing Course'. It's still in its box. You see, I wanted to write *my* book, not someone else's sanitised version of what a book should be. Cocky or what?

I started reading *Eat, Pray, Love*, to see if I wanted to emulate her writing style, but it was too full of angst for my liking. On impulse, I picked up *Bridget Jones' Diary* and thought, 'Yes, this is it. Funny, quirky, and written in diary form. Fandabidozi!' That book was my inspiration.

I learnt a lot about self-belief along the way. I learnt to go on my gut instinct rather than follow other so-called experts like sheep. When the lady I employed to edit my book sent my first edited chapter back reading like a Jane Austen novel, I had a hissy fit. Rachel calmly exclaimed, 'It's only a book, Mum. You haven't got a life-threatening illness. Chill out!' It was then that I realised that this book was very much 'my baby', written in conversational slang, in my voice, and I didn't actually want a single word changing, just a spell check.

For the front cover, I was told I should use a company which had lots of different designers all competing for my business. This was great, as they all had different ideas. Unfortunately, a lot of them didn't read my specification, which led to much hilarity as I realised just what young designers thought 50 looked like; the most memorable being two people crossing a zebra crossing with a zimmer frame!

Some of the designs were really imaginative, but just didn't seem to have that wow factor. After lots of humming and ahhing, I realised that it was much more personal and powerful to use a photo of me and Rachel in a human pyramid with fellow travellers on Whitehaven Beach, Australia with its turquoise sea and white sands. Perfect! Once again, I reverted back to my gut instinct and what, in my heart, just felt right.

Once you've opened Pandora's box, you can never put the lid back on. Alleluia!

Since writing my book, I've had to get out there and do lots of public speaking and newspaper, magazine and radio interviews, which would have filled me with horror previously. Now, I see them as fun! I also had to undertake several challenges to publicise it; I went on a 15-mile off-road bike ride, shot down a zip wire at 'Go Ape' and went fire walking on hot coals, amongst other things (and survived!).

Once you've written a book called *Life Begins at Fifty*, you have to really *live* it, so I write a regular blog (www.lifebeginsatfifty.info/blog) and jump at every opportunity going. Over the last few years, I've travelled solo to New York, been skiing again after 25 years, enjoyed house-sitting in Spain, flown to South Africa to visit a friend at 5 days' notice, and last year, I visited Australia, Vietnam and Abu Dhabi. My mission is to inspire people to get out there and really live rather than waiting for a rainy day that never comes. Live each day as if it's your last…because one day it will be!

Tips for Self-Belief and Confidence

1. Think of something you've always wanted to do. Visualise yourself at the end of your life and ask yourself, 'Will I regret not doing this?' If the answer is YES, look into ways that you can make it happen, e.g. if you want to travel, can you house-sit, take early retirement, work via a laptop, take a sabbatical, look for a new job? List all the pros and cons, and if the pros outweigh the cons, start making plans. Believe you can! Once you start following your dream, the universe conspires to make it happen.

2. Our state of mind affects our perception of life. When we're feeling low, we tend to believe our negative thoughts, which can lead to apathy. We make excuses as to why we can't change our lives for the better. We question our self-worth and confidence, and this holds us back. When we're feeling happy and carefree, we still have negative thoughts but realise that they are just thoughts and take no notice of them. In this happy state, we make good decisions, 'go with the flow', embrace life, and feel excited and positive about our future. So, make decisions with the right mindset and go with your gut instinct. It never fails!

3. Walk the talk. Confidence and self-belief are achieved by first of all pretending that you have those qualities. Obviously, I wasn't feeling completely confident about getting into a dinghy and flying over a 7-metre waterfall, but I just kept telling myself I could. Once you've achieved something you thought you couldn't, your self-esteem soars and you realise that anything is possible. You really are so much more than you think you are.

Helen Carver is an author, public speaker, wedding celebrant, estate agent, property developer and general lover of life. Since writing 'Life Begins at Fifty' and creating her blog, both her daughters married, which inspired her to become a wedding celebrant. Just after she had qualified, one of her best friends, due to start working in an estate agency a week later, experienced a traumatic brain injury. Helen, with 25 years of experience in the industry, stepped in whilst she recovered... and is still there. Helen loves the camaraderie with her hilarious work colleagues, and keeps her cool whilst her clients are invariably losing theirs, when coming across problems with their house sales. Despite a few health issues, Helen's friend has made an amazing recovery, and they are considering writing a book together to give hope and inspiration to others in a similar situation. Watch this space... www.helencarvercelebrant.co.uk

THE GRAND CANYON

I teeter on the brink.

The majestic chasm
Gapes gloriously
Around me;
Breath-taking, expansive;
Its rock-bound brilliance
Stillness personified.

Aeons of spiritual wisdom
Etched in sentient strands
Densely crown
Stalwart outcrops
of Colorado-carved canyon.

Gazing anew at pure grandeur,
Poised; staring into the abyss,
Strains of glorious greatness
Stir stubbornly within my chest.
Engulfed with the wisdom of the elders
I contemplate pure bliss.

Eager as the eagle,
My soul and senses soar,
Launched into the vastness,
No longer at safety claw.
Recklessness reverberates
As I release a MIGHTY ROAR!

Sue Williams

Go On – I Dare You!!

Irene Brankin

'There is no passion to be found in settling for a life that is less than the one you are capable of.'
— *Nelson Mandela*

I CAN ASSURE YOU that life isn't over when you find yourself saying 'what's the point' when you are in middle age; dealing with the various losses, changes or happenings that generally come around then, whether major or minor.

I have been a prime example of this and could actually say: 'been there, done that, got the 't' shirt.' I am sharing a part of my story that I hope will let you see that we are not in control of our lives but it is up to us to see that we have a choice in what we do with it.

I have been perhaps where you are now and, in my experience, this can be a cyclical experience. It can happen again and again in different forms. It is more about how we deal with those times of losses, confusion, change and even the fear that occurs.

Here is a part of my story: -

I was someone who was always saying to herself, 'There has to be more to life than this!' and I would say that this has been my lifelong quest, as well as to enable others to find their own answers to this question.

This striving brought me to Essex, after growing up in a working-class family in Glasgow, to return to studies. I ended up as a Chartered Counselling Psychologist running and teaching various groups - self-development, counselling and supervision while mentoring others.

To all intents and purposes, my life was fine – healthy, in a supportive marriage with one son, and fulfilled in my work of enabling others to address their potential. It was a good midlife even if filled with stressful juggling of a lot of balls in the air.

Without going into the reason, I chose to resign from my Training Organisation as I trusted my own decision making. This caused me to have all that goes with it, the feelings of abandonment as I had to also let go of the many titles I held.

It was a really distressing and tough time for me (even if it had been my choice) as all the losses connected me to my feelings of loneliness, tears, sadness, anger, fear and financial worries.

However much I girded my loins to move on, it did not happen for me. I eventually realised that I needed to be in this place of mourning in spite of the feeling of fighting in a paper bag, going nowhere, except becoming exhausted.

One year after my resignation, I was diagnosed with bowel cancer. Again, a time of shock and trauma, although in a different way – it was definitely not by choice!

My body reacted very badly to one dose of chemotherapy, and I ended up in intensive care for two weeks while they were fighting to save my life.

On eventually leaving the hospital after another eight weeks, I decided not to work with people any more as I considered I would be struck off for telling them, 'You think you have problems?'. I only returned eventually to my supervision work.

While getting my strength back, I slowly became aware of how many women were forgetting about themselves as they were putting others and their work before themselves. Somehow or other, I decided I would write a book which I thought about giving the title, 'The Call of the Wise Woman' but eventually chose 'The Visible Woman: More Lust – Less Must.'

My book was in response to my anger at observing what was happening around me. So many women appeared to be wasting their life away through not listening to their own inner voice, their loss of self and the pain this caused them. Too many women were not living life as they could and were afraid to become visible by not allowing themselves to be their own person.

The book also talked about how the media encourages age discrimination, and how we collude with them by telling ourselves that 'we are too old', or 'it is too late to make changes in our lives' and so we feel we have to stick with what we know.

What gave me the confidence to be 'back out there again' was simply getting off my backside and doing something – taking steps towards my dream of being visible. I knew that I still had so much wisdom, experience and maturity to be of service to the world.

Before returning to work with women, I challenged myself by writing this book in my 50s (and I have written another since), and I can assure you that it was definitely challenging.

I only know that it is so important for women like you to be role models for other women to follow, and to let them see that there is no right or wrong way to be or act in life. It is all about being yourself and allowing the rest of the world to see you in all your uniqueness – wherever and however you do this.

Life is about re-connection with yourself and your dreams and following through with them.

Whatever is going on with you, it is important to listen and re-connect. It is imperative that you follow through with these covered up dreams or else, you will become distressed in some way. Isn't it always better to try even if there is an element of fear, or if it doesn't work? You will have learned what to do the next time. You may have forgotten that fear and excitement are two sides of the same coin, so choose the latter.

When you do this, I can't promise you that life will change overnight, but I can promise you that you will be so proud of yourself for expressing the gifts you came into this life to share. Somehow, you know that it is not about staying in your comfort zone. Of course, yes,

I stayed there for a long time to return to good health and chose what I did with that time while waiting to hear that voice saying, 'it's time now.'

I needed that space to listen and perhaps, that is what you will need to do, and then your inner knowing will tell you when it is your time to move out from your comfort zone into the challenge and excitement of the unknown.

You will re-discover your lust for life and that you don't have to conform to the rules that were once accorded to chronological age (women in midlife). You will find that you can be young enough to get more out of life, old enough to have your life experience to draw upon, and mature enough to laugh at life and yourself. As you will know, laughter is good for the soul and for those around us to share it with.

When you include more of you and share your gifts, you will know that life is a walk in grace, and to grasp that there is inherent goodness, which is sorely needed these days.

Enjoy being you.

Here are three suggestions from me -

Even when you are afraid, breathe into that Wise Woman inside you who knows you are more resilient, stronger and more courageous than you think you are.

Remember it is always Both-And, not Either-Or, and so do not to be afraid to own your vulnerability as well as your strengths as they make up you.

You can become exhausted by using your precious energy to hide 'you,' so why not simply put it to good use and do whatever it is you have always wanted to do!

Irene Brankin is an Essex girl, via Glasgow and a wife, mother, "Nana" to two grandchildren and an all-round surprising woman. She is a Chartered Counselling Psychologist, Mentor, Supervisor, Group Facilitator and Author who has worked over mainland Europe, particularly Sweden. She believed she could live a life she loved on a number of occasions and went for it through life's trials and tribulations. She is now more content than she has ever been.

Irene's opinion is that you need to have the courage to be yourself, listen to your own voice and laugh a lot at life – have fun. Find Irene at: www.thevisiblewoman.com

A BEGINNING

A small chrysalis
Cold dank darkness is her life
Suddenly she feels warmth
A glimmer of light

She stretches and pushes
The shell-like tomb cracks
Fear of the unknown awakes
And keeps her still

She is safe in her darkness
But dreams of hope and light
Light was there at the beginning
There is knowledge that she can fly

A sense of encouragement
Pervades this moment
She is not alone
The universe needs her to fly

The dark cask opens
The light shines
She stretches out her wings
Today she flies
Elizabeth Beetham

So, What Are You Fighting For?

Joanna Derby

'Trust yourself.
Create the kind of self that you will be happy to live
with all your life. Make the most of yourself by fanning the
tiny, inner sparks of possibility into flames of achievement.'
— Golda Meir

'YOU FIGHTER YOU!' As soon as my friend said it, I realised that I had inherited all of my mother's traits.

As a child, I was quite an extrovert, happy by nature and always surrounded by friends. My mother, who was loving and caring, was a real fighter. A single mum with two girls, she had been brought up in a different culture. Still, she had the resilience and drive to fight the system on almost every occasion: she didn't always win, but in hindsight she gave me the same determination, the belief that you have to fight for what you want in this life. Boy was she right.

I have literally lost count of the many battles that I have faced. However, I want to give you a snapshot of some of the career transitions I have contended with using sheer resilience, determination, self-belief and by literally having the confidence to ignore other people's well-meaning advice.

My first clear memory of my mum fighting on my behalf was with the education system. We lived in a town where the secondary schools were structured in a three-tier system, Grammar, Technical and Secondary Modern. As you can imagine, places for the first two schools were very competitive. My sister had obtained a place at the Grammar school (so no pressure there then) and when my 11 plus test came, with no preparation, tutor or parental support, I completed it in record time. Proud of myself I checked my answers, looked around smugly and sat there watching everyone with their heads down still trying to complete the paper. After a while though, something just didn't seem right... and with twenty minutes to go I realised that there was an hour-long essay question on the back page!

My next vivid memory connected to that awful 11 plus, is of sitting at the back of an office with my mother who was forcefully arguing my case to go to the Technical School. I think I was only a couple of marks off the entry point, and I remember her sadness when she was told that I would be going to the Secondary Modern. I knew I was going to the 'sink' school and I knew the implications that would have for my future; but at least I would be going with my friends. Therefore, I embraced my new school. See, I told you I was a happy and resilient child. I think they call that having a growth mind-set in this day and age.

Incidentally, what I didn't tell you was that we were the only black family in the town in those days. From my recollection, that came with a multitude of issues. Issues for me, but mainly issues that everyone else in the area seemed to have about me and my family. To the point where I used to walk past people in the street and after I had passed them, I would turn back round - always guessing correctly who would have stopped to stare at me. I developed an instinct for picking them out and rewarded them by sticking my tongue out at them. Yep, I was quite brave - or stupid – and, just for the record, adults weren't immune either. At that age I really didn't understand the possible repercussions of my actions. It was the mid 1980's and there were numerous race issues at the time.

Oh, just one more thing to give you an idea of how I grew up, then I really will move on to share some of my decisions around career transitions. In my Year 7 class, I sat next to a boy who was really 'ok' for a boy and we got on pretty well. Things drastically changed however when I moved house, and ended up living on the same street as him. He never spoke to me again.

However, to be fair, we had more pressing problems to deal with: namely the excrement that was thrown at our living room window. And, not just the once... Watching my mum scrape this stuff off our window and wondering when it was going to happen again, or if it was even safe to go outside was probably the lowest point of my life. Yet my mum took it in her stride and dealt with all the external pressures so that we didn't have to.

There was much more going on but as I only have a 2000-word limit I had better stop there! However, you get the gist - we were a single parent black family living on a council estate, albeit a fairly nice one.

Anyway, off I went to the Secondary Modern School and had a great time. As I was the fastest runner in the school, I was a bit of a celebrity and the boys who mattered made sure that I wasn't bullied at school. Academically, I always studied and worked hard and developed a real competitive streak. Education and school became my comfort blanket. I learnt via my mother, on a daily basis, that this was my way to beat the system and have a better life than her.

I used to keep my school reports in a drawer and look at them nearly every day, literally counting again and again how many 'A's I had received. Ok, so I was at the top of a pretty poor performing school; but that was good enough for me. So, when I was assigned my careers appointment slot, I felt well prepared with my entry requirements to become a nurse: knowing that if I worked really hard I could do it. It took just one sentence to quash my hopes and dreams - 'we have a lot of care homes in this town, you could become a care assistant' my careers adviser said.

This, for me was the catalyst that made me realise that I would have to fight against the systems that were there holding me back. I got an awareness of 'know your place' loud and clear. No discussion of becoming a nurse. This school really had defined my future prospects. Finally, recognition of why my mum was so sad in that education office became a sudden sharp realisation for me.

My sister helped me to study for my exams. The day the results came through the door I was sitting, nervous with anticipation, on the floor waiting to catch them. Tearing the envelope open; I needed four grade ones. There was no opportunity to take 'O' levels at our school - the highest grade you could get was a CSE with a grade one - equivalent to a grade C at 'O' level. One, two, three, four… I counted again, one, two, three, and four. I was ecstatic! Although I didn't achieve a grade one in English or Science, I knew that at least I could go to college and get onto a national level course.

I had fought the social mobility battle and I had partly won; the feeling was good. Education wrapped itself around me again and the warmth and comfort it gave me provided me with even more resilience.

Jump forward many years and against all the odds, and many similar battles, I now have two degrees, two post-graduate qualifications, and a highly professional career behind me (alongside two kids). Yet, I find myself dressed up in a chicken suit dancing to Gangnam Style whilst trying to entertain a party of 30-50 kids with a colleague. My eyes flicker around the room, and although I quite like playing the clown, I feel as if I am being looked down upon by all the adults, inwardly thinking 'poor woman is that her job?!' I am sweltering in the outfit. My husband thinks the whole party host thing is a waste of money (so no support there) and my mummy friends snigger at me when I stand inside a supermarket trying to get people to sign up for parties (so no support there either then).

Yeah Jo, so just what are you doing? Not enough time to explain here.

Jump forward further in time and I find myself cleaning the floors in school as part of my Teaching Assistant role, even though I have an MBA. Add to that the fact I was told that I would never get into a Russell Group University to do my teacher training (by a jumped-up Teaching Assistant). However, ironically that little 'chicken experience' has held me in good stead to get a place on the course. Never give me a challenge, I feel like saying to her. I am resilient, I have a growth mind-set, and most importantly I am a hard worker with a fighter instinct. All of this has led me to: -

1st career tick – I am a qualified Careers Adviser (yep making sure that other people's beliefs and aspirations are not crushed)

2nd career tick – Teacher Training QTS (making sure that the teaching is good for others to ensure social mobility)

3rd career tick – Working for myself as a Career Coach and helping others to recognise and action their dreams and work vision …

So here I am now. Finally, with the 'belief' in the knowledge that the best decisions are made when you know who you are (self-awareness) and where you want to be. The belief that you have to be strong enough to ignore the noise from all the other voices around you, as their perception of what they want you to be or do could be completely different to yours. You have to overcome those limiting beliefs that hold you back, those etches ingrained in your brain that hardwire you to conform to what society expects you to do. Instead, practise a 'growth mind-set' approach and ignore the many who resist change and question you from their fixed mind-sets (believe me there are many).

You have to be brave in making decisions and taking risks: it is ok to fail at things (I have on many occasions and, like me, you will learn from your mistakes). You have to think outside of the box sometimes, oh, and most importantly 'network'. For years I missed out on this trick as no-one ever told me the opportunities it can bring.

Networking can make your life so much easier, although, as I lacked confidence in myself it probably wasn't my first 'go to' strategy. But now overcoming this limiting belief and working with my extrovert personality style, I have even been able to take this opportunity to write my story for *'Believe You Can Live a Life You Love at 50+'* which came about through networking. So, believe in yourself as no-one else can do it for you.

I would highly recommend the following:

1. Please take a Myers Briggs Type Indicator personality test, or one of the many others available. It really has changed my life. Until you know yourself, how will you be able to interact confidently with others, how will you understand why you act in certain ways in certain circumstances? Spend time getting to know 'you,' your

strengths, weaknesses, values and goals within life. It will enable you to make happier, more confident decisions.

2. How resilient are you? Do some research around growth and fixed mind-sets. Work out which one your friends or family fall into. This will enable you to see who is more likely to support you in any new endeavour.

3. What are your limiting beliefs and how can you overcome them? We all have them. Spend some time thinking about what it is that seems to hold you back. Consider how you could address that. Then whatever the world throws at you, you are in a better position to cope.

For me, being self-aware is the key to contentment and happiness. I have stopped fighting now. Care to join me?

Joanna Derby is a part-time teacher who also runs her own coaching business. Her work decisions are made in relation to her whole family identity. By this Joanna means her new-found identity, work identity, and her roles as a mum and wife rolled into one. Previously, she saw 'me' as more prominent, and over the years, one role may have had a slight precedent over another. Over time they finally began to merge. Although she can laugh now, Joanna found certain periods of her life painful and confusing. She remembers being annoyed, angry, excited, and positive about the many steps that she has chosen. Now, all of it finally makes sense and she can appreciate the new "me". This makes any steps she now needs to make crystal clear. www.pro-ceedcareer-coaching.com

MIND AND BODY

Mindful of the time
The pink rolled mat calls
It waits in the car's boot, curled neatly in a roll
It smells of sweat, fear and pain
What is there to gain?

The mind resisting the need
Shall I not bother or should I go?
The battle proceeds with fervour
But I know I need this
It heals my body and mind

Entering the hallowed hall
There is hardly room for me
Spreading the mat brings me ease
Lying eyes tight shut; waiting to begin
Listening to my laboured breathe

The teacher speaks in a quiet calm voice
I strain to listen and lose myself
Body momentarily hesitates
Not wanting to move
Then it begins
Like an automaton I unwind

The movement becomes me
Lost now in the need to stretch and strengthen
Wanting to be supple, toned and young
Mind and body now as one
Yes, I'm really having fun

I love my yoga class!

Elizabeth Beetham

Finally, Fit – Forever!

Julie Hobbins

"How you look at it, is pretty much how you will see it"
— Rasheed Ogunlaru – Life Coach, Speaker, Author

HAVE YOU EVER felt that you would like to be fitter and healthier? And be able to *stay* fit and healthy for the long term? Maybe you've got some lovely clothes in your wardrobe that are a bit too tight for you to feel comfortable in, or perhaps you get out of breath using the stairs at work – and end up going into meetings huffing, puffing and red in the face?

Possibly you know that you've got into poor eating habits, you know what you should and shouldn't be eating, and how you should be exercising, but you can't seem to stop yourself. And potentially, you suspect your weight could be contributing to other health problems…

Where would you rather be instead? Imagine if you had boundless energy and could easily run and catch that bus or train? And what about the feeling of knowing that what you are eating is keeping you healthy, and curing disease, not creating and feeding it.

And what if you could get into those lovely clothes in your wardrobe again, or even be able to buy new ones in a smaller size – and look and feel great when you see yourself in the mirror?

Picture having the confidence to wear what you want, eat what you want, do what you want, and most of all BE who and what you want to be.

Well that's what I want to tell you about. My journey from overweight, frumpy, shy and retiring office worker, to where I am now – full of confidence about my future, taking some bold steps into the unknown, and with a healthy outlook in every sense of the word.

Where it all started...

Step back in time with me now to one of those long hot summers in the 1970's. I'm about 8 years old, sitting at the kitchen table, literally gagging and retching at the pungent smell of the food in front of me. My mum is standing over me, her frustration apparent on her pinched face as she pleads with me "Julie love, you have to eat something – you must get some nutrients and vitamins if you want to grow up into a strong and healthy girl." I'm what you might call a picky eater, and most foods seem to make me gag involuntarily. I want to please my Mum and Dad, but I just can't eat the food they want me to.

It's now a few weeks later, and I'm outside in the sunshine with Mum while she is picking vegetables from our vegetable plot in the corner of the garden. She's teaching me how to pick the ripe green pea pods from the plants, and I curiously pop one open to marvel at the big fat round peas inside. Mum urges me to try one, so I pick one out tentatively and am suddenly amazed at the explosion of taste and sensation as the sweet fresh pea bursts in my mouth. Wow!

Somehow that was the turning point for me. I started eating, recognising and enjoying the healthy homegrown vegetables, and gradually exploring other taste sensations and all sorts of other foods as well. My parents were obviously delighted to see the change. So much so that they continued to praise and encourage me to eat as much as I wanted, of anything and everything, and so I did! What little girl wouldn't respond by doing more and more of what brought such lavish attention and loving reward?

Let's fast forward now to the late 1980's and I'm about to head off to university – but instead of the excitement of my future unfolding before me, I'm really reluctant to leave the comfort and security of my home with familiar faces around me. I've grown from a scrawny child who couldn't eat, to a fat and frumpy teenager in drab, baggy grey clothes that I wear to disguise my figure, shy and lacking in confidence, and scared witless of what the next few years would bring.

Is that the way you would want to be starting such an exciting new phase in your life?

My impetus to change

It's now 2016. I'm in the doctor's surgery and waiting for him to tell me the worst. Have you ever been given some potentially devastating news that could turn your world upside down, but at the same time, proves hugely motivational?

"Mrs. Hobbins, I'm sorry to say..." the Doctor peers at me over his spectacles, "that although the news is positive today, if you don't address your weight issues permanently, the next time you won't be so lucky. Do you realise how much obesity contributes to heart disease, cancer, high blood pressure, diabetes, gout, ... need I go on??" It feels to me like he is almost sorry I *didn't* have one of these illnesses, but it's the impetus I need to turn things around. I make a decision there and then, that I'll find a way. I'll lose the weight, and I'll keep it off this time. I'm not far off my 50th birthday, and it feels like a major milestone that could go in one of two directions. I want to be able to enjoy the rest of my life and my later years, not find my health deteriorating and hindering me.

You see, I'd tried lots of different diets in the past, including Atkins, Dukan, Weightwatchers and Slimming World. I had more success with some than others, but none which I managed to maintain once I'd lost the initial weight. And more often than not, when the weight crept back on, it was more than when I started. So, I guess I was the typical yo-yo dieter. But all that was about to change.

I came across an online programme, seemingly at random, but now I wonder if there were greater forces at work. I signed up, despite what seemed to me to be an exorbitant cost, but a little inner voice kept asking me, "Can you afford not to?" I was also worried about how much time commitment there would be – I'd done other diets before which only worked because they had become all-consuming and everything else fell by the wayside – and that clearly wasn't sustainable. This one included daily food reporting and felt like it could go the same way.

The difference for me in this journey was undoubtedly the support of my personal tutor, from both an accountability point of view, and from the way she helped me to really see things in a different light. She never criticised, even on days where my eating was not the best, and she helped me to understand that I needed to be gentle on myself, and not beat myself up for poor choices or decisions.

I learned to look inside at what I was eating, and more importantly why I was eating, and make the gradual changes in habits that made this approach both easy to do, and simple to make permanent. It was much less about the food I was eating and the exercise I was taking, and more about small incremental changes in my mindset that influenced what and how I ate and exercised. As I came to believe that I could make these small changes easily, consistency grew, and the next steps became easier and easier each time.

It was at this time that I realised the impact of my early eating habits as a child, and how these had become a reason for me to eat more and more to foster the love and approval of my parents.

While I say some of it was easy, it wasn't necessarily a walk in the park (although I did start to do more of that to make sure I was getting daily exercise!) I gradually learned about and understood the impact my busy lifestyle was having – juggling work, family, friends and my health. I saw how that was impacting on my stress levels, and with that came the realisation that holistic self-care was really what had changed in me, and what made this approach work for my weight, my attitude, and my plans for the future. For example, during a particularly stressful and challenging time at work, I was able to apply the same mindset approach to address the overwhelm, which helped me to see things in a better light, tackle things in a calmer way, and ultimately achieve more.

Feeling the benefit

I lost 26kg in ten months, exceeding my target - that's just over 4 stone (57 lbs.). I'm now within the healthy range for my Body Mass Indicator for the first time in years. I've dropped 3-4 dress sizes, and I have so much more energy that I just randomly run upstairs at work, something I would never have even contemplated before. And I know that I don't have to "stop dieting and gradually reintroduce normal foods" again – the way I eat and think about food now is the way I can and will eat and think for the rest of my life. So, it is completely sustainable for the long term.

There are no feelings of depriving myself, guilt, or any other negative thoughts. And I enjoy all the food I eat slowly and mindfully – eating has become so much more enjoyable. My outlook on so many other things in my life has changed too – all for the better, because of what I learnt on my journey of self-discovery.

I've realised that each of us has far more control over ourselves, our environment and our lives than many of us realise, and I've decided that this is far too important to keep to myself. Each step of my weight loss journey was based on a small choice to make at each step of the way, and each choice was mine alone. And more importantly, the reasons that had prevented me from both recognising that I did have a choice, and from making the right choice, were not necessarily real or true.

Just because I'd put weight back on after previous diets, didn't mean I'd put it on again after this one. Just because I associated a large bag of crisps and a glass of wine as a vital part of the evening's "entertainment" while watching a film on Netflix, didn't mean that I couldn't wean myself off that habit and retrain my brain to think, "I don't do that anymore".

Often, we stop succeeding at something because we have a minor setback and then stop trying at it. Keeping going, just one step at a time is still making progress, but in much more manageable chunks.

You could call this awakening a discovery of self-belief, but it felt like a much subtler journey than that – more like a gradual lightening of the sky at dawn than a "light-bulb moment".

So, I've been spreading the word among friends and family, and now decided to train to be a health coach. I've launched my own business helping others to find the confidence, and their own solutions, to achieve their weight loss goals, and potentially their bigger dreams and aspirations as well… and to get finally fit, forever! I am delighted that I'm now helping others to achieve what I did, and I already have some very satisfied clients.

So, my three exercises to encourage you to believe in yourself and realise the power and control you do have over your fate, are below. Feel free to look at these in the context of weight loss if that is something you are aiming for, or from the perspective of achieving any goal, dream or desire that you may have now, or have had in the past, but aren't really convinced that you can achieve it.

1. If you are struggling to accomplish a goal, ask yourself what part of you doesn't want to achieve it. Dig deep, and you might find that part of you is scared of the outcome. Perhaps it might alter your identity; either how you see yourself or how others see you. Does this take you out of your comfort zone? Is it safer for you to stay in a known place, even if it's not where you want to be, because the unknown is scarier? If that's the case – really check what you are scared of. Picture the worst-case scenario, and think what you could do to mitigate that, if it were to occur. Try considering taking action as an exciting experiment; yes, it could fail, but you would learn a lot if it did fail, and who knows, it might even work!

2. Be more mindful, particularly around food – always! Enjoy and savour each and every mouthful before, during and after you eat it. This not only slows down the speed at which you eat, it gives your body more time and space to register when it is full, and it adds a huge amount of enjoyment, happiness, and satisfaction to your day. When you eat like this, it is also much easier to stop when you reach that sensation of fullness. Scoffing a chocolate bar and then

wondering where it went doesn't create any satisfaction, and leaves you just craving more.

3. When you eat something you feel you shouldn't, or do something that you wish you hadn't, give yourself permission to analyse why you might have done this – without feeling guilty, being critical or beating yourself up for it. Be kind to yourself and just seek to understand whether you were trying to avoid doing something else – whether it be an unpleasant task, or conversation, or as a way to avoid a negative feeling of some sort. Whatever it is, just give yourself a moment to really think about what you were trying to avoid, and then ask yourself – if I was an expert in ... what would I do in this situation? If it feels right, you can then take that action, or you may come up with something you can do to make some progress towards this "expert" action. The key is to take some action. And the great thing is, the more you start doing this, the more chance there is of you getting to this point before you eat or do the "wrong" thing, and you'll be able to address a different problem at the same time.

Julie Hobbins runs two businesses – one is a successful skills and further education consultancy, and the other is her fledgling weight loss coaching business; Enlighten Me Weight Loss Coaching. She supports mainly women in their 50s to find the tools and confidence to transform their bodies and their lives. Find her on Facebook at Enlighten Me Weight Loss Coaching, or www.juliehobbins.com

WEIGHED DOWN

Why don't I clear my closet?
Let go of coat and hat;
Bag up saggy trousers,
Other appalling old tat!

A congestion of clothes;
Ranging from small to extra-large.
In danger of choosing the wrong ones,
Spoiling my décolletage!

Why don't I clear my closet?
Once sylphlike, wore many a transparent gown,
Long since I've expanded,
Prefer to stay under my eiderdown!

Will I ever diet,
Return to being slim?
Strangely, all that's missing,
Are clothes to wear to the gym!

Why don't I clear my closet?
Declutter, make ample space?
The minute I stop simply dreaming,
My future wishes will gather pace!

Sue Williams

Sink or Swim – It's Up to You!

Karen Ramirez

"Our deepest fear is not that we are inadequate. Our deepest
fear is that we are powerful beyond measure. It is our light,
not our darkness, that most frightens us. We ask ourselves,
who am I to be brilliant, gorgeous, talented, fabulous?
Actually, who are you NOT to be?"
—*Source - Marianne Williamson from her book "A Return*
to Love: Reflections on the Principles of a Course in Miracles"

I STARTED 30 NOVEMBER 2016, my 50th birthday, with a sense of utter dread, combined with resolute determination. My friends and family had planned lovely events for me to celebrate, yet I felt stressed about my business. I was also conscious that I'd hit 50 having spent the majority of motherhood as a single mum of two going from month to month feeling pulled in every direction (albeit with a present, supportive 'Ex').

On that day, I had a serious business meeting to attend and I walked out of it thinking, right, time to take life, the universe and everything in hand!

That's a pretty tall order when you're starting below par. Where do you begin?

I'm a firm believer in getting the basics right first – for me this boils down to eat well, sleep well, take exercise and get fresh air every day.

WAIT! Before those of you who hate exercise or think this is going to be about diets turn straight to the next chapter, I would stress that:

1. I have never dieted per se – and never will!

2. I believe health and fitness is as much about mindset work as diet and exercise;

3. I believe that IT DOES NOT MATTER WHERE YOU START, just take the first step!

Still with me? Let's go!

On 30 November 2016, I wasn't UNFIT, but I felt wrung out, my head was spinning and I knew that taking my life by the scruff of the neck was the only option for the year ahead. I had just secured an ongoing contract that gave me (i) an adequate level of financial security and (ii) the ability to take time out from relentlessly looking for new business.

I took December 2016 out to step back, recuperate, fulfil contractual obligations but not take on any more. In addition, I went through my diary and cancelled the majority of the work Christmas parties that I usually attend and which required travel and high levels of networking and alcohol consumption!

Instead, I focused on eating healthily, early nights, not drinking too much (although Christmas and New Year were 'well-celebrated') and getting myself energised and motivated ready to hit January at a run.

A new year brings an avalanche of resolutions which invariably start to go 'off the boil' by February. Running and hockey have been 'my thing' for a few years and were regular features in my week, but I felt that in this 50th year of my life, I wanted to challenge myself, push a bit harder and feel a greater sense of achievement... and Lent was on the horizon...

I'm a great believer in giving up something for Lent, and having felt the benefits of reduced alcohol in the lead up to Christmas, I decided to give up alcohol completely for Lent. The first week or so was difficult, but then it started to feel 'normal', and the results showed in my skin, my running and my mood. I came up with a new business idea, and my new-found energy allowed it to develop.

Around this time, I was following the fitness journey of two women slightly younger than me, but who had started out less fit and who were clearly doing something that was delivering great results. They looked energetic, healthy, glowing – and I wanted a bit of THAT!

By May 2017 I had joined the same group and coach as those ladies. It was a leap of faith – for logically, the programme they followed made no sense for me.

The coach, David King, is based in Austin, USA, so how could he possibly coach me here in the UK and get results? All his coaching was delivered online so I was highly skeptical about whether I would really do what was required and whether it would work if I did.

The coach put out an offer: become part of my tribe, get yourself one of my 'Fitness Stalkers' for two weeks, follow what I say, participate fully in the online groups and it will work!

I signed up. This coach has unwavering and infectious levels of energy and enthusiasm, and values mindset work equally alongside food and physical exercise.

It was he who introduced me to Hal Elrod's *Miracle Morning* to start my day. He who introduced me to tools such as an 'Anchor of Discipline' (for me, 5 x 10 squats, sit ups and press ups, EVERY SINGLE DAY) and an 'Anchor Goal' (usually a special event for which his clients want to look and feel their best).

I've never met anyone with such skill and passion to motivate from thousands of miles away.

By the end of May 2017, when I packed the car for our annual friends and family camping holiday, I felt fitter and in better shape than I had in my 20s. Mentally and physically. And everybody noticed!

A new sense of confidence and excitement was taking hold. In my twenties, I'd enjoyed swimming, usually after a night of salsa dancing and whisky sours on a tab with friends in London. I started swimming again, loving the feel of the water on my skin and the stretching and toning of new muscles as I did so.

July 2017 heralded the tenth anniversary of the death of one of my cousins in Afghanistan. He was just 22 years old with a great future ahead of him. For his parents, sisters and brother and our extended family, I wanted to mark this anniversary to show that he hadn't been forgotten.

Encouraged by a friend who is an experienced open water swimmer I registered for a 2.5km swim in the open sea, and committed to raising funds for my cousin's regimental Benevolent Fund.

It's fair to say, I'm not a great swimmer! I can only do breast stroke. I'm very slow. However, I knew that I had three things going for me:

1. I CAN SWIM (so it wasn't entirely a standing start)

2. I live in a city with amazing sporting facilities and so there is no reason not to train at least for the distance, if not the stroke technique.

3. My open water swimming friend introduced me to a flooded quarry set up for diving and open water swim training.

Having told my friends, and committed to my family and my cousin's regiment that I would do this, there was no way on earth I was going to let them down!

Discipline was required, and for me that meant taking the training seriously. I made sure I swam at least twice a week, increasing the distance slowly throughout June and July.

I went back to zero alcohol – and the reactions of myself and others was an education in itself. There was one day in particular that stands out and which clinched my resolve.

On Thursday 22 June 2017 I made a trip to London with a series of meetings and events to attend. The first was a 50th Anniversary Lunch of an organisation with which I am involved, held at the House of Lords, starting with reception drinks and followed by wine with the meal and a mid-afternoon meeting in a bar with a colleague.

The day finished with 'drinks' with another friend and colleague for a 'catch up'. When I arrived, he jumped up to greet me with a hug, a kiss and 'Dry white?'

His incredulity when I requested sparkling water verged on comical! At this point, I was hit by two realisations. I mentally added up how many glasses of wine I would have drunk that day had I been on 'business as usual' – and it was too many. I also recognised that I had 'Sobriety Guilt' - I felt embarrassed about 'confessing' that I wasn't drinking.

There's a happy ending to this day. After the initial incredulity, my friend asked me about the swim, was curious to know how I looked so great (his words, not mine) and asked why I wasn't drinking.

He then commented: "You know what, Karen, that's amazing. I'll tell you what – next time we meet, let's not do the 'drinks thing', but I'll sign you in at my gym, we'll go for a swim and have a bite to eat afterwards instead."

We did – we do – and I doubt even now that he has any idea how much that level of support meant to me! No trying to 'turn me' or make me feel like the 'party pooper' – just friendship that respected and supported my goals.

In August, I headed to Devon with my friends and our daughters for the 'big swim'. I felt so nervous tears pricked in my eyes. We started; there was a decent swell and some waves were breaking over my head. At one point, the safety paddle boarder asked me if I'd like a tow. I declined, but asked if I was actually moving forwards – she assured me I was, and both she and my friends stuck with me as I completed the entire swim, finishing roughly third from last.

Seeing our daughters waiting on the quay as we arrived was priceless, and the short run from the quay to the pub was worth it for the best-tasting pasty and pint ever!

Since that day, my health and fitness fluctuate marginally. However, I keep them within a self-imposed range. I am still in the best shape of my life, and this has had benefits not just physically but in terms of quickly identifying new opportunities in my professional and personal life.

As I write, it is January 2019 and I have announced my intention to complete a full alcohol-free year. After that, I may never go back – who knows?

Since my 50ᵗʰ birthday, I feel I have a thousand stories to tell. Not just mine, but those of people who watched and contacted me about their own stories, hopes and fears of being ridiculed.

My advice would be to just go for your goal! Share it with someone you trust. My experience is that most people don't laugh, they support.

Sometimes achieving your aim just needs a different approach. When my son was just eight years old (he's now 21), his hockey coach set up a weekly family hockey session that I subsequently ran for several years. It's still going and welcomes men, women, boys, girls; all levels from almost-beginner to county and league level players. I've seen mums and dads join having not played since school. Some have progressed to join a 'Back to Hockey' programme and then been accepted alongside students in their late teens/early twenties to play in club teams.

As I write this, just yesterday, a new lady arrived having never played before – and I'd happily bet that this time next year she'll still be playing! It's all about how you make people feel.

So, what have I learned that I can pass onto you?

1. Set yourself a goal – but combine it with a reason to achieve it that touches, moves and inspires you.

   Plan out what you need to get there – a business or lifestyle coach, friends to join you, cheerleaders to keep you going when you least feel like it.

2. Start your day right! Get up early enough to establish a morning routine and get clear about the day ahead.

   For me, it's Hal Elrod's LifeSAVERS (Silence – Affirmations – Visualisation – Exercise – Reading – Scribing), taken from his book *The Miracle Morning*.

3. Prioritise. Whether it is a task or a goal, the things you make a priority are the things that will happen. For me, hockey on a Saturday morning and running on a Sunday morning are sacrosanct.

Above all, take your health and fitness seriously. Without it, everything else is, at best harder work, and at worst will prevent you living the best of your life yet.

Karen Ramirez is the founder of Sporting Sheroes, an initiative that champions women in sport, from grass roots through to elite level. Karen speaks Spanish and French, and has worked in a number of multicultural and international organisations.

Karen is a past chair of the *Association of Women Travel Executives* (AWTE) and is listed on the Women 1st *Top 100 most influential women in hospitality, passenger transport, travel & tourism*. She is a senior management member of the *Cross-sector Safety and Security Communications hub* and in 2015 was awarded a Commendation by the National Counter Terrorism Policing HQ for her work in a national business engagement campaign. Contact Karen on keramirezuk@gmail.com. 07887 942578

SHINE FOR ME

As you remember me this day,
Let sweetness blend with sorrow,
You are my gift,
Left on this earth,
To create a brighter tomorrow.

And, as you ever blossom and grow,
My legacy lives on;
So be my light,
Within this world,
Through you, still brightly shone.

Sue Williams

Good Grief

Karen Robinson

*"In short, health is measured by the shock a person can take
without his usual way of life being compromised"*
— *Moshe Feldenkrais*

I T WAS A cool, dry November evening in 2007. The lull before autumn
slides into winter. Seven young people were heading to town in
two cars. My eldest son Luke, only twenty years old, was a backseat
passenger in the blue Renault Megane racing ahead. His younger
brother by two years, Jake, was in the car behind.

The stillness of that Monday night was only disturbed by their
excitement. It was gone midnight. A light breeze was whispering
through bare branches. The Renault driver showed off without a care,
feeling invincible in spite of several appearances in court for dangerous
driving.

The adrenaline that at first had fuelled Luke's fun now turned
to stone in his belly. His shoulders tensed as an unpleasant memory
surfaced… the funeral of a friend.

"Slow down mate," he called out. "I know two people who died on
this bit of road."

Too late.

The driver lost control. It took just over two seconds for the car to
come to an abrupt halt in the hedge the other side of the road. Nose to
tail. Nose to tail.

BISH.

BASH.

Luke was catapulted through the smashed windows.

His neck torn open.

Arms flailing.

The weight of his head leading the way to the hard surface of the unforgiving road.

BISH.

BASH.

THUD.

Airbags had burst into life and saved the two cousins in the front. Unable to open their doors they climbed out of the twisted car through the sun-roof, but Luke was not there.

"Luke? LUKE!"

As the second car arrived on the scene, slowing down in disbelief before stopping, Jake jumped out and ordered the driver to pull off the road. He could see the other crumpled car and hear his brother's name echoing in the night air

"LUKE! LUKE!"

An eerie calm fell as he heard the others calling out. It was one of the girls who'd found Luke on his back, twitching, but not conscious, his life soaking away into the road.

"What can we do?" she cried to no one in particular. Desperate for someone to do something. To take control.

"Don't move him." Jake's reply came firmly. He remembered you shouldn't move people after an accident unless you have to and he already had his phone in his hand calling an ambulance.

Within minutes the sirens screamed into the darkness before the blue flashing lights became visible. Two young police officers arrived at the scene already full of adrenaline from the rush to get there. One tried to resuscitate Luke, the smell of iron and stale cigarettes accosting his nostrils, while the other demanded to know what had happened.

Bawling at Jake he couldn't hold back his anger,' 'Do you realise your brother is probably going to die?"

Other emergency vehicles arrived and whilst everyone was taken away in ambulances and police cars, Jake sat alone at the side of the road, hanging onto hope until finally, another police car was arrived and a policewoman confirmed that Luke was dead.

Whilst my elder son died on the road and my other son mourned his loss, I was blissfully unaware of what had occurred and slept on for hours, not hearing the phone ringing, over and over again. Finally, at around half five in the morning, my stepfather let himself into our house just as my husband had come down. My husband's gentle hand on my shoulder woke me from my too short slumber.

"You need to come downstairs."

I flew down the stairs, not feeling the supports under my feet and I stood in the living room waiting to hear what I already knew in my heart.

"I'm afraid Luke's been in a car accident," he said.

"Is he dead?"

"I'm afraid he is."

Immediately a strange feeling raced through my veins, my muscles weakened, and I wanted to collapse in a heap and never get back up again. Waves and waves and waves rose up from my belly as tears sprang uninhibited from my eyes, until I managed a breath.

'What do I need to do?"

"Come to the hospital with me."

Nothing prepares you for the death of a child or the unfairness of things happening out of order. Seeing his beautiful face, dark eyelashes brushing his cheeks and feeling his warm hand it was hard to believe he wasn't alive. As disinfectant mixed with the smell of body fluids, I stood sobbing.

"My boy. My son," was all I could manage.

I felt completely helpless. If I hadn't known I had a choice (and some do say ignorance is bliss), I could have just given up. But I already knew I would get through it somehow. I knew I was strong. I thought that's what people expected of me. But being strong turned out to be different to what I had anticipated.

On the journey home, wondering how I was going to get my other children through this, my inner voice spoke.

"Take care of yourself first."

I was already living a very healthy lifestyle, but I'd had some unsettling symptoms in the last couple of years with IBS and fatigue. Taking my inner voice literally, I allowed my grief and tears to flow unrestrained for two days until my youngest sons, aged just nine and seven, asked to go back to school and alarm bells began to ring. The situation was too intense for them.

Whilst I knew I needed to release the powerful emotions I was feeling and that it was healthy to do so, I also had a fierce desire to protect my children, so I decided to stop crying in front of them as much as I could. I didn't know at the time that *not feeling* was my default. The more shut down I became, the more in control I thought I was. The more I shut down the more disconnected I became from my body. The more disconnected I became from my body, the more my physical symptoms increased.

Seeking support, I sent a collective e-mail to all my contacts asking for help and pouring out my heart as I tried to make sense of what had happened. I thought it would be an easy way to explore my thoughts and feelings, but became self-conscious about writing to them, embarrassed that they might think I was being self-indulgent. I turned to keeping a diary instead. I knew that 'one day' I was going to write a book. I had wanted to since I was a teenager but had never had the courage or felt that it was important enough. There was no sudden epiphany, just a quiet inner knowing.

Over the following few weeks and surrounded by a community that I hadn't even known existed, I felt completely loved and accepted, even though all of my emotions were exposed as I swung from grief to anger and to joy. I was unconditionally loved because I had been through one of the worst experiences a parent might go through. I laughed and cried in equal measure. I spent more time with my parents, step-parents and extended family than I had for years and I was thrilled to be in their company again.

We shared stories of our experiences with Luke and at times what a little bugger he'd been. Open, heartfelt conversations that filled me up and made me feel fully alive. I listened to music that Luke used to love and sang my head off unafraid of getting the words wrong or singing out of tune. It was empowering; but it didn't last. Life goes on. People go back to their busy lives and I was left alone to get on with mine. I went through the motions doing all the things that mothers do and quietly dying inside.

This numb out and shut down pattern was reinforced when, eight months later, my beloved brother was killed in another road crash and four months after that my uncle suffered the same fate. I screwed down my own emotions even tighter. I still believed I had to be the strong one and though I had nothing to give, I gave anyway. Crushing my own grief and tears killed my spirit. Although I was never suicidal, I sometimes felt it would be easier to just curl up and die, but a part of me wouldn't let me do that.

The next five years I now refer to as the lost years. I continued to do my duties as a wife and mother but there was no spark left. Life became pointless. Flat, drained and lacking any enthusiasm, I went through the motions but felt no joy. If it hadn't been for the tender administrations of my osteopath husband, I would have been a complete wreck.

Eventually it was my deteriorating physical symptoms that prompted me to look for solutions. I went down a number of expensive rabbit holes without finding the miracle I was looking for. It wasn't until I began to admit how crap I felt, in spite of the brave face I was putting on, that I was able to find a practitioner who helped me get to the root of my health issues and start to feel free again.

I discovered that in the early years of my life I had decided that *it wasn't safe to show my emotions and I had to hide them from other people because they didn't know how to deal with them.* This decision had unconsciously become a core belief that was now running my life.

The problem with suppressing the nasty, uncomfortable feelings is that it's not possible to suppress them without also blocking all the fantastic, joyful and the glorious enlivening ones too. The calm and in control exterior that I had been portraying was hiding decades of trapped stress and trauma in my body. What I thought had been resolved (and what made me strong) was just hidden and locked into my body chemistry. This was the beginning of releasing and letting go of all that stress and feeling alive again.

As I began to recover, I had four false starts at writing my book. A year into my 50s, I was diagnosed with a minor skin cancer which freaked me out for a while. While I waited over four weeks for the diagnosis it gave me time to think. I realised I was most likely over half way through my life. What did I want to do with all the knowledge, skills and experience I had accumulated? How much time did I have? What did I really want to do with that time?

Then I came across a belief that has completely changed my perception.

Your relationship with the problem, IS the problem.

I wrote it down and carried it around with me for weeks and weeks. During this time, I realised that my perception of writing a book always seemed like a luxury or an indulgence I couldn't afford to spend time on. It isn't a guarantee of getting published, being paid or putting food on the table. Almost everything I'd ever done in my life had had to have a practical outcome. But… none of us know how much time we have and believing this I had missed opportunities to nourish and nurture myself in a way that filled my heart and energised me.

Having made my book a priority everything began to fall into place. I found the perfect mentor and group for help and support. Ideas flowed to me like a river and I am now well on the way to finishing and publishing a self-help book.

Who I really am is a creative, emotional, funny, caring, responsible and practical woman. I don't have to be one thing or the other. I can have it all by embracing the whole of who I am, not just the parts I thought were acceptable to everyone else. I can feel and express difficult emotions and still be loved. Being strong means allowing myself to be vulnerable.

I now believe that the most important thing in life is to be fully expressed, to experience the whole rainbow spectrum of our emotions and to follow our natural impulses and urges. To do that, most of us need to release old trapped stress and trauma that got stuck in our bodies. Then nurture our nature by remembering, re/discovering and embracing the things that light us up and make us feel buoyant and alive.

The greatest gift we can give our loved ones is to be who we truly are, not some version of who we think we ought to be to fit in. To be who we truly are means to feel everything. To feel is to thrive!

How to Help Yourself

1. **Pause and Connect to Support.**

    Pause now.

    The bottom line is we all need to feel safe.

    As you read this, begin to feel the connection of your body being supported by the furniture, the floor or the ground that you're on. Drop your attention into the connection between your bottom and your chair or feet and floor. Skin to fabric. Bone to surface. Allow yourself to be fully supported through your whole weight. Pause and do this regularly throughout your day.

2. **Rediscovering Your True Self**

    Grab a pen and paper. Take your time with this. Come back to it if you need to. Allow yourself to be completely honest and see where it takes you. Finish off the sentences below. Free write until there's nothing left to come out. There is no right or wrong.

    Experiment with writing with your dominant and non-dominant hand.

    I would most love to feel…

    My heart/soul/spirit/mind would love to…

    My inner child longs to…

    I feel at my best when…

My whole body is longing for/to…

I feel envious or jealous when I see/hear other people …

If I had no fear, I would…

You can play around with these yourself and make up your own.

Read through and see where there are common threads. You may want to take a break and come back to it after a few days. This can help with clarity.

Apply. Start to bring these elements into your life. Bit by bit. Day by day.

3. Following Your Nature

When you were born you used sounds, crying, yelling, farting, sneezing, slapping your lips, peeing, pooing, coughing and a whole range of biological impulses to get your needs met. Over the years most of those things somehow became unacceptable, not polite or even rude. Ignoring natural biological impulses puts a strain on our bodies, makes our bodies wrong and stunts our natural expression and creativity. From today bring your attention and awareness to your system and find out what it naturally wants.

Eat when you're hungry and stop before you're too full.

Pee when you feel the first impulse to do so.

Rest when you feel tired.

Stop before your body hurts.

Say 'no' and mean it.

Cough, take a breath, sneeze, stretch, fart, belch…

Now notice, over time, how following your biological impulses every day impacts your life in a positive way.

Karen Robinson is a Self Care Empowerment Coach, Peaceful Warrior, Writer, Relaxed Nature Lover, Wife, Mum and author of the upcoming self-help book: **Release Revive Thrive** - untangle yourself from stress and make inner peace your lifestyle choice.

Find out more: www.karen-robinson.com or join the free Self Care for Caring People Community.

LOCKED AWAY

Buried deep, locked away,
Secrets, silence;
So much to say.

You are a beacon,
A being of light,
Yet you've lost your voice
Given up on the fight.

You are a miracle about to be reborn,
You are the shoe, not the shoehorn;
Fighting to make everything fit
When there's no end, no container for it.

Release true essence, unleash potent power,
Joyously all around, gentle raindrops shower.
Cascading down, caress soft, fertile ground,
With a wondrous, ethereal sound;
The clarion call of the newly crowned.

Sue Williams

This is My Time to Thrive

Linda Barbour

'When you start seeing your worth, you will find it harder to
stay around people who don't.'
—Unknown

M Y SELF-BELIEF DISAPPEARED slowly but persistently over 25 years of marriage. Silent criticism and judgement, a lack of care and appreciation gradually chipped away at it. Like many people who lack self-belief, I also lost my self-confidence and self-esteem

I became very self-critical, anxious and depressed and constantly doubted myself.

Despite my achievements as a good mother and wife, building a successful therapy practice and having good friends, I never felt 'good enough.'

In the years leading up to my 50th birthday it came to a head; I had no idea who I was, or what I wanted to do. I couldn't see a way out of my situation.

I was no longer the party animal I was in my 20's or the career orientated woman I was in my 30's. I had spent my 40's being a wife and mother, but my children were growing up and preparing to leave home; my husband and I were unhappy together, despite all my efforts.

On the outside my life looked great. I was living the dream – married, residing on a small farm, eating home produced food with two wonderful healthy children. I was surrounded by beautiful countryside to ride through on my long yearned-for horse and doing a job I loved.

But on the inside, I felt like a total failure. I tried to ignore these inconvenient feelings for a while, hoping fervently that they would go away. I agreed with what other people were telling me – I 'should' be more grateful and appreciative of what I had.

I concluded that there must definitely be something wrong with me because I wasn't happy - other people had much worse lives after all. I believed that it was me who was the problem that needed to be solved. Questions churned around my mind: -

- Maybe it was the menopause, or that I needed to do more self-care?

- Maybe I needed to attend to my spirituality or financial wellbeing?

- Lose weight?

- Be fitter?

As time went on, my self-belief, self-confidence and self-esteem continued to seep away. I lost my sense of self, felt depressed and constantly weary. My efforts to **'improve'** myself, mould myself and make myself fit in made me feel worse and not better.

I needed to do something radical if I was to get out of this rut.

I took a year out of my practice to focus on myself and what I wanted to do next, using up all of my savings. I did things I enjoyed outside of the family and spent time with people I loved and who loved me. I read numerous self-help books, did courses and worked with several gifted therapists and mentors. To my surprise, everything I did led me to the same conclusion. It wasn't me that was the 'problem', but the situation I had got myself into that was causing my difficulties.

Eventually the penny dropped. I realised that there wasn't anything 'wrong' with me. I wasn't to 'blame' and I felt the way I felt - no matter how other people thought I 'should' feel. The problem wasn't 'me', rather that I had lost belief in myself. I had stopped trusting my feelings and I was constantly beating myself up for thinking the way I did. I put others views of me ahead of my own and lost my sense of self as a result.

The depression, that I hadn't admitted to - because how could I as a psychotherapist be depressed - gradually lifted.

I stopped believing that:

- I was the problem that needed fixing - 'if only I was different, everything would be okay'

- what other people told me about who I was and how I should live my life was right

- if other people were happy, I would be too – I came to realise that they <u>were</u> happy, but I wasn't

- my unhappiness and failure to love my life were my fault. I felt that I was not understood, loved, respected, appreciated or valued; I was bound to be unhappy in those circumstances

I started to believe that:

- I was a worthwhile person and was loveable just for being me

- I was the one who could make myself matter and feel important

- I needed to rediscover who I was and what I wanted

- I had nothing to prove to anyone else

- My feelings were a message to me and I had to trust and listen to them

- That is was ok for me, even with all the knowledge I possess, to be in the situation I was, and to stop beating myself up for all the mistakes I thought I had made

To begin with, changing my beliefs and the way I saw myself was incredibly discombobulating. My brain had no idea how to work out how I really felt, what I wanted, who I was now or what I needed to feel fulfilled and happy. I had to stop worrying about upsetting or disappointing other people and learn to listen to my heart and mind again.

Getting rid of my accumulated negative feelings about myself has meant that I am now clear about who I am, what is right for me and the people that I love.

Like many women I had put caring for other people before caring for myself. I am very intuitive and empathetic and the messages from other people about how they felt became louder than the messages from my own mind and body. Ignoring and not believing and trusting myself led to my depression and deep unhappiness.

My journey with self-belief has been a journey back to myself, to trust and believe in myself and regain my self confidence and self-esteem. For me having self-belief has been about learning who I am now, how I want to be and not just about what I am doing.

Most of all, I have learned that to believe in myself I had to discover how to value myself, make myself matter and that what I want and how I feel must matter to me.

Therefore, I had to change my situation. After 25 years I regretfully left my marriage, my home and the life that I had invested so much time and energy into. I had 'served my time.'

I built a new life supported by an amazing group of friends and family who have helped me in every way imaginable. I left behind those people who are critical of me or only wanted me for what I could do for them. **This is now my time to thrive.**

Using my expertise as a psychotherapist, coach and small business owner, along with my own personal experiences, I have made a commitment to dedicate the rest of my professional life to helping other women to believe in themselves.

Since then, I've worked with many private clients, spoken in front of countless groups: I am creating my dream life – being happy in my skin, building my dream business as a coach and psychotherapist working with women in their 50's and beyond, to reinvent their lives.

I have created a 3-month programme and a one day intensive to support my clients. These are based on the 6 steps you need to take to get rid of the blocks that keep you stuck or overwhelmed. Learn to replace those unhelpful beliefs and feelings so you can believe in yourself and feel happy in your skin. Once this happens, achieving your dream lifestyle becomes not just possible but easier too.

Making changes on the inside means that you develop self-belief naturally and when this occurs you also have the courage, clarity and motivation you need to make changes that you know are right for you – and more importantly, that last.

Steps to change self-belief:

This exercise will help you to understand the link between your beliefs and your behaviour.

What am I likely to say and/or do if I believe the following?

- Things don't generally work out for me

- Things generally work out for me

- People like me

- People don't like me

- It is not ok to ask for what you want

- It is ok to ask for what you want

Now write down one way in which you behave that you want to change and state the underlying belief behind it.

To change a belief, you have to prove both it and yourself to be wrong. Look for evidence to disprove your belief rather than looking to prove your belief e.g. take the belief you stated above, or use "I will never be good enough" as this is one that is commonly held.

- Notice the times other people say you are good enough, give you a compliment or positive feedback and take it on board.

- Notice all the things you do that are good enough and write them down in a daily TA DA! list.

Instead of having affirmations or positive self-talk, ask yourself powerful questions - this is where the magic begins!

Set yourself a goal and write it down. Then ask:

- What beliefs would you need to hold to achieve this?

- What beliefs would stop you from achieving this?

- What beliefs do you hold that you need to change?

- How will you find the proof you need to change your beliefs?

- Who can help you?

Notice when you do something different to what you would normally do and enjoy the ride!

Linda Barbour – Therapeutic Coach

We all want to be happy. By using her 20 plus years of experience and a combination of ground-breaking knowledge, skills and approaches, Linda is committed to helping you to achieve this. Practical help is not enough. You need to change from the inside to make meaningful changes in your life.

Linda's results show that by getting to the root cause of your difficulties and using helpful tools and strategies, you can achieve the most extraordinary success quickly.

Described as 'life changing', 'caring' and 'gets amazing results' by her clients, Linda is committed to helping you make changes that last.

Visit Linda's website for free resources and blogs full of tips and tools, or to find out about her coaching services: http://lindabarbour.co.uk/

WE GATHER

We gather, loud and proud. No longer bowed
down by the weight of centuries.

We cry, we weep, emotions seep from care worn crevices,
sweeping away scars and woes.

She knows her time has come,
She knows she must beat her drum and dance till dawn.

Forlorn no more, reborn to adorn mother earth's grassy plateaus,
With open arms she sweeps, sways, embraces life.

Sue Williams

Hidden Gifts and Silver Linings

Louise Hatch

'You have to believe in yourself. That's the secret.'
— Charlie Chaplin

L IFE CHANGES CAN appear out of the blue. In my case, at age 45, I experienced sudden onset tinnitus, or as it is commonly understood, ringing in the ears.

It began during a car journey. I had been sleeping in the passenger seat to try and alleviate a migraine headache that had been troubling me all morning. I woke at my destination to alarm bells, which I initially thought were outside my head, but quickly realised were internal sounds.

The ringing continued unabated for a few weeks, so I went to see my GP, where I was referred to the Ear, Nose and Throat department of my local hospital for a check-up and hearing test. I assumed at that point that I had an infection, nothing more.

How wrong I was.

A few weeks later I was seen by the consultant directly after my hearing tests and checks were carried out. I went to his office alone, assuring my friend that it was all a routine formality and therefore, she waited in the main reception. I sat down, primed to be told of an infection that I second guessed to be the cause of these latest developments.

The consultant turned to me, put my audiogram results down on the desk and said, 'I'm sorry to inform you that you are deaf'. I stared at him, hard, and immediately began to argue with this highly respected, experienced hearing professional, 'Deaf? I can't be! I can hear you! You've got this wrong.'

He then proceeded to cover his mouth with his hand and continued to speak; his words became indiscernible – it was then that my world turned. I could barely make out what he was saying.

He removed his hand and explained gently that I had begun to unconsciously rely on lip-reading. He assured me that what the test results revealed were indeed the case and went on to prescribe two hearing aids for my congenital, bi-lateral, sensorineural hearing loss.

I don't remember too much of what he told me after that.

I stumbled through panic–stricken questions. I was a singer, could I still sing? What about my music projects?

He said I should be able to continue, and that the tinnitus may make things harder, but not impossible. I left the appointment stunned, in shock and in tears. A lovely nurse made an appointment for a hearing aid fitting and then walked me back to my friend – who recalls me stumbling through the reception doors ashen faced as I began to take in this new-found knowledge.

Over strong tea in the hospital cafeteria with my friend Kate, I began to have tiny light-bulb moments, reflecting on past experiences of mis-hearing nuances of conversations, the tv being on super loud, the difficulties I had been facing while recording vocals with headphones on, and the ongoing health problems I had been experiencing for several years resulting in stress and overwhelm. It all began to make sense.

It was later explained to me that struggling to hear can be exhausting, and I had often felt tired to the point of despair. I couldn't quite believe how I had lived this way for so long without knowing, and yet, how would I have known? I had adapted to the missing frequencies thus far and until the tinnitus began, I had managed. But this potent messenger heralded a new phase of life.

As I began to come to terms with my diagnosis, I soon realised that continuing in music to the level I had been previously was not going to be possible. I was fearful of making my hearing situation worse. Although my hearing loss is static rather than progressive, fears at that time were not logical and therefore I had developed an almost phobic reaction to loud sound, hyperacusis, and my stress levels rocketed!

I finished the recording project I was working on, providing the vocals for a New Age/Classical album, and I hung up my singing hat. I admit at that point I was lost. For some considerable time, I entered a dark phase, grieving the loss of my old life and depression took hold.

During these challenging times I had been fitted with my hearing aids. I recall my whole body giving a big sigh of relief as the first one was switched on. It was my first glimpse of a silver lining. My system finally felt supported, the listening effort reduced over time, and gradually over the coming months my energy levels improved, so too my general physical health.

I had begun to do my own fervent research pretty soon after the discovery of my hearing loss and ongoing tinnitus. I linked in with two main charities who offered information and support. I also returned regularly to my very kind audiologist who then referred me to a tinnitus specialist. I learned during that consultation that currently there is no cure for tinnitus. It's a case of managing it, by distracting the brain from focusing on the internal ringing sounds via various means such as gentle sound therapy, utilising the hearing aids fully and combining relaxation and mindfulness techniques. In time 'habituation' would happen. I was also advised to greatly reduce my time in loud noise and in silence. I left that appointment in hopeful spirits.

I began to look for other outlets for my creativity. As well as being a singer for many years I am a lyricist and songwriter. It was to the medium of writing, my first love, that I returned. Although a quiet activity, during those times at my desk the ringing seemed to almost disappear as I focused on the words and the flow of writing.

I signed up for an online creative writers' course, feeling nervous and completely out of my depth, but something in my heart knew I had to take this step. Looking back, that decision was a turning point.

I rediscovered the power of the written word. The healing aspects of the inner world of imagination and expression were a balm to my weary heart. I forged on.

As I grew in courage, my next step was to go on a writing retreat. At this time, I had no concrete plan, just an inkling of an idea for a new business formed from a discussion with a close friend over coffee by the river one evening in Greenwich where we both live. We talked of how 'one day' we would like to have a retail shop that celebrated women on all levels, body, mind and spirit, a fusion of our shared passions for fashion and spirituality. It was with these thoughts in mind that I headed to Devon's beautiful countryside.

The seed of Dragonfly Lifestyle was well and truly planted on that trip. I didn't realise it at the time, but the wheels were in motion. It was October 2014.

Fast forward one year, and in October 2015 we opened the doors on our new business and shop! The universe provided the wind to the sails, and at times my friend Jules and I felt that all we could do was keep up, keep working and keep the faith!

Eighteen months into the business and I realised that my hearing needs were changing. The countless customer interactions, event planning, phone calls and day to day running of a successful boutique required more listening effort. So, I made enquiries into the private sector for hearing aids, as a wise friend advised at the time – 'if your business needed investment you wouldn't hesitate, so why are you not investing in yourself and your health?' Point taken, I made an appointment with a new audiologist and I tried out and then bought a top of the range pair of hearing aids. I experienced a marked difference instantly, the nuances I had missed were lessened and once again my energy levels were restored.

My audiologist Adam Chell and I became friends. We shared similar values for hearing healthcare, and shortly after meeting one another, Adam invited me to a tinnitus support group where he was the guest speaker. I hadn't been to one before and I found the like-minded connections and shared experience so uplifting. He and I took that inspiration and decided to set up our own project Tinnitus Rooms, part of which is a free tinnitus support group based in Greenwich, working in conjunction with the British Tinnitus Association. In 2017 we both attended their Tinnitus Advisor Training Program and their Group Facilitator's workshop.

Each step of the way I have come face to face with my fears and my own self-doubt, not least when I was asked to feature in a video filmed by my hearing aid company as an example of a hearing aid user, sharing my experiences of hearing loss and tinnitus. Professionally filmed at Dragonfly, it pushed many buttons for me. Not only would I be heard – I would be seen! My hearing loss experience was going viral. I had many a sleepless night as the nerves nearly got the better of me, but I decided that it was time to step up and use the platform to help others.

I remember how devastated I felt in the early days of my diagnosis. I lost not only my hearing but my long-term relationship, my music career, my confidence and myself. It was time to maybe make the road a little easier for someone else who might be struggling as I once had.

The video was well received, and I grew stronger in my self-belief by taking that step. I went on to speak publicly at the hearing aid company's shareholders meeting in central London some months later. Again, sharing my experiences, but this time in a very corporate setting in a 5-star hotel.

I was literally sick on the morning I was getting ready to leave. It had tapped into my childhood memories of being chosen by my teachers to be the one to always speak at assembly, event days and Christmas specials. Some of my peers didn't take too kindly to me being in the spotlight, and I was bullied incessantly because of it.

I believe something takes over us when we are on path and aligned. The fears get laid to rest when we are being true to ourselves and our service here. If we can, we push through despite those fears, even though they can seem overwhelming at times, a new sense of what is possible emerges.

I entered the hotel conference room and a peace descended within me; I surrendered to the moment. I had prepared well, and I knew I simply had to trust the process. And you know, strangely, I have never felt more at home than when I am doing this work. The key for me is the more authentic I allow myself to be the more connected I become. It's a blessing.

Almost 11 years on what have I learnt? I've learnt that within each adversity somewhere there is a hidden gift. That in every seemingly enforced change there are silver linings. In every fear, there is a lesson and an opportunity to build on our self-love and self-care, enabling us to be fully present for others when they need it the most.

I would like to leave you, if I may, with these thoughts:

It's about moving...

From isolation to connection

From depression to acceptance

From being frightened to being empowered

'Perfection does not exist, authenticity is eternal'

My best to you

Louise x

Exercises

Positive and Kind Self Talk

We can encourage ourselves with the words we say in our heads or we can diminish ourselves. The choice is ours.

*Start to notice the impact of self talk on the way you feel, the things you do, your interactions, your confidence level, your health and wellbeing.

*Catch the voice – the internal dialogue – is it useful? Is it kind? Is it empowering? Is it even ours?! Sometimes we take on the old external dialogues we heard as children and you may be surprised to discover they are no longer relevant to you now.

*Talk to yourself as you would a child that needs support or a close friend that needs reassurance.

*Write positive statements on notes around your home and work place. Let them be external reminders to check the internal voice. Make it your friend. Work with it. Have fun with it. Empower yourself with kindness. Start with yourself and notice the changes.

Find Your Passion and Follow It

It could be that the passion you felt for things as a child has got lost in day to day life, and those expressions need rekindling. Perhaps, you feel that you have never known what your passions are? If so, start to explore what makes your heart sing. It can be the simplest things or the most diverse, and it will be unique to you.

Finding those with similar passions is very life affirming, and energy can build brilliantly when collaborations flow well and succinctly. This is a wonderful chance to explore. Remember, the key factor is, how do you feel? Alive? Inspired? Energised? Natural? Peaceful? At 'Home'? These are good indicators that you are connecting to your heart's passions.

Writing

Write simply for yourself. I have found that committing a plan to paper gives it life. So be careful what you wish for! In all seriousness, there is a magic to committing to the page or screen. It's like the universe is listening. Also, writing can be prophetic. We write and we discover. We write and we clear space in our minds for more positive self talk and passion finding, and for dreams to break through.

Choose your medium. Pen and journal. Keypad and screen. Talk into a voice recorder. It's time for you. It's time to voice your thoughts and in doing so you may be surprised to know the deeper expressions you hold, the gifts below the surface. The heart of the matter.

And most importantly – enjoy it.

Louise Hatch is a writer, fashion retail business owner, tinnitus group facilitator, and hearing healthcare ambassador.

Louise has trained as an NLP Master Practitioner, Reiki Master, Vibrational Healer and Tinnitus Advisor.

She lives and works in the beautiful World Heritage Site of Greenwich, London.

Her friends and family mean the world to her and she credits them all for being the 'wind beneath her wings' in times of adversity and triumph. www.louisehatch.com www.dragonflylifestyle.co.uk

www.tinnitusrooms.com

FIFTY PLUS

Your time has come at 50 plus,
Perhaps too young for free pass for the bus,
yet primed and ready for the ride,
unlock the fear you have buried inside.

Set off on the open road,
no longer cowed, chafed, or goaded,
suitcase unpacked, rucksack loaded,
follow the signs, not yet derailed,
this time experience happy trails.

There are no boundaries to your journey,
be free, explore, let loose in a gurney!
Smile, and wave as you explore,
venture through that open door.
Heal the past as you rest in nature,
let go of any annoying nomenclature.

Open your journal at a clean new page,
write as if a seasoned sage,
of the life that you will lead,
let it flow, no stress impedes
your creative musing,
now's the time to live
a life of your own choosing...

Sue Williams

Courage and Clarity are All You Need

Lynda Holt

"Show up, be brave and do what you believe in"
— Lynda Holt

URNING 50 HAS been an interesting milestone. Physiologically as women we are moving to a different phase of life. For me this also coincided with changes in family roles – sharing my home with two young men, where rather than me having control looking after children, life is much more of a partnership.

I'm also caring for increasingly frail elderly parents. Those relationships are changing too; where my father has been my life long rock, he now needs my help in looking after his affairs and in his daily living. While I feel very privileged to have these opportunities, it kind of brings with it this evolution of generational responsibility, stuff that, honestly, I don't feel ready for. I'm not ready to lose my rock, I very much still feel I need his wise counsel and I'm certainly not ready to move into a 'third age' role in the family.

I entered my 50's, grappling with the "M" word – and the psychological impact of changing hormones is equally as powerful as the physical changes. Yes, I've felt foggy, questioned myself, been forced to consider how I cope with changing energy levels, but in my head I'm still the same passionate young woman, with the same will to do good in the world, and need to have made an impact. I guess we have two choices, we sit back and coast through life or we live it. I believe I've always lived rather than coasted, but turning 50 has created a sense of urgency.

Often when we coast through life it is because we lack clarity about what we want, or we lack the self-belief to make it happen – the latter becomes so much easier to fix when we are clear about what we want life to look like and why that matters to us. One of the most powerful exercises I undertook a couple of years ago was a 20-year life plan – yes it was weird, I kept thinking I'll be knocking on 70 how do I know what life will look like, in fact I'm not even sure I want to think about what life might look like. Guess what, the clarity that came from that exercise has enabled me to achieve more in the last 18 months than in the last five years.

In 20 years, I want to be part of a connected community of brave people each doing their bit to enhance the world we live in. I might be in my 70s, but I still want to teach, to speak, to write, as well as to enjoy my family – hopefully my grandchildren, and share my wisdom to future generations. I want to have my health, be able to still enjoy riding, travelling, photography – you know, I'm really lucky, I love my life, I don't want to stop doing stuff as I get older.

That means I have to act now to create the future I want. Remember that sense of urgency I talked about? It was this exercise that made me realise if I wanted this brave community I had to get on and build it, now! If I wanted to be known for my commitment to bravery, not in the hero, adrenaline junkie way, but in the everyday stand up for what you believe in, do good and be connected sort of way, then I need to start playing bigger, quickly.

When I look 20 years out, I see myself leading a group of physical communities, multi-generational hubs where people share ideas, work together, and develop businesses that support a world of collaboration and contribution over competition and criticism. Idealistic? Yes, very and in my world view also possible if we have the courage to connect. The way humans connect has changed exponentially over the last 20 years and may well do the same again over the next 20, but I don't believe we will lose the need or desire for face to face interaction.

So, when I looked at my 20 years vision, I found myself asking 'What am I waiting for? Why have I not started to build these communities now? Why am I not talking about connection, courage and contribution? The answer was simple – it's scary, putting your life mission out there. Balance that with I'm 50 and if I don't start now it's not going to happen – which is worse? I'm successful, I have a great life, I do work I love, that makes a difference and I have so much more to contribute – this was it, my wake-up call. If I don't start acting instead of dreaming, I am going to run out of time.

With this in mind I got a shifty on, I ran BraveFest, my first annual business festival, in 2018, the first Brave CoWork – my 'one day' project, has just opened, and my next book – talking about courage and connection, is just submitted to my publisher and will be out in 2019. I believe it was clarity of vision and purpose that has made this happen – this stuff matters to me more than fear, risk of failure or ridicule, or popularity. The thought that I will drift through the rest of my life without making my contribution is too painful to conceive.

20-year life plan exercise:

Here's how it goes, and I suggest you give yourself a couple of hours to play with this.

I liken this to mountain climbing, you can usually see the path to the next peak and while you are in the foothills you can see the higher peaks, but not always how to get to them – this is what your 20-year vision is about. No one expects you to have a detailed plan for life in 20 years, but you do need a broad vision of what you'd like it to look like.

Start with the 20 years vision – how do you want to be spending your time? Are you travelling? Looking after grandchildren? Do you want to be still working? What do you want to be known for? (This can be anything, practical wise woman, inspirational entrepreneur, a specific contribution to your community – or the world, someone your family can depend on to always be there – it's your vision you choose). Think about why this is important to you, this will help you define or refine your values, and how you craft your life moving beyond your 50s.

This 20-year span is probably the hardest bit – it calls on you to look at what you have accomplished so far, where you are holding back and playing small, and frankly where you have sold out on yourself and settled for less than you are here on this earth to do. If you are having trouble committing, or daring to scope out your life in this way, remember this is your concept, your vision, you can change it if you want at 1 year, 5 years or if life throws you a curveball any time. The trick here is to have some direction, some focus for your unconscious to work with, some reason to dispel some of the self-doubt that may have held you back in the past.

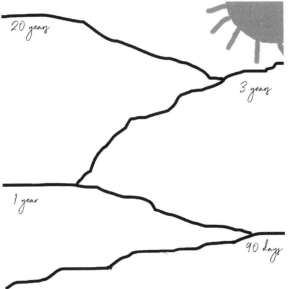

Once you know what life looks like at 20 years out then work back, where do you need to be in 3 years – this may still be conceptual, using my example I need to have at least 2 co-working spaces open, a media profile following the book launch and to have a strategy in place for looking after my health and maintaining my work/life balance and family commitments. I'm a bit fuzzy still on the exact path as I can't yet see it, it's the peak over the horizon.

Coming back to one year out, that is much more tangible – you should be able to see that path, plan your journey and know what the milestones along the way are. Again, these are your markers of success or progress, you get to choose what is important to you, what is challenging and achievable in just one year. Understanding what you are prepared to do and more importantly what you are not prepared to do is critical here, if something feels off, it probably is and you probably won't do it.

I then break my year into 90-day chunks – these I plan in detail. Ask yourself what your next 90 days looks like, what are the 1-3 things you need to accomplish to move you towards your year plan. I never put in more than three so that I can maintain focus.

I hope you had fun with this exercise as well gained some insights about the greatness you still have to share beyond your 50s.

Clarity is important, but only part of the picture. Belief in your ability to deliver on this vison is critical. Yet for many women this is the hardest bit. We tell ourselves so many stories about who we are, what we can practically do, what we deserve, about not being or having enough, that we can paralyse ourselves into inaction or conformity. Often these stories simply become our favourite excuses for not showing up, for not being brave and for not doing the things that matter to us.

Until you get focused on your excuses you are destined to keep making them. One of my favourites is– I'm too busy. In life that shows up as - I can't write another book until…, I'll open the first co-work when…, and as soon as I got connected with my excuses, I realised how ridiculous they were. The I'm too busy mantra was quite literally keeping me stuck in busy and disconnected from my life mission.

What are your favourite excuses?

Simply spend some time focussed on the reasons and default excuses you give for not doing something you find scary, or you don't want to do. Grab a piece of paper and jot them down, all of them!

Any surprises? We make excuses to keep ourselves safe and to reinforce the stories we tell ourselves about who we are, what the world is like and what we can do. If your stories are empowering you, give you the confidence to take action towards what you want in life then great – if they don't you might need to change a few.

You might be saying easier said than done – and I'm not saying it is easy to change life-long patterns or stories, but if they are not helping you have the life you want you owe it to yourself to make the change. Try this exercise for deconstructing unhelpful stories.

Change your story:

In the excuses you listed above there will be a few underlying stories, pick them out one at a time and ask the following:

Is it true?

Does it serve me?

What do I need to believe?

Sometimes a story may be true, for example I love to travel, I can also get motion sick on a swing! Is the story true – yes. Does it serve me – no. What do I need to believe – that I'm ok, even if I feel unwell on the journey, I will be ok when I stop moving, the reward will be worth the discomfort. How do I change the story? By constantly reminding myself of the experiences I've had exploring new places, how enriched my life is. The first story is still true, but I'm focussed on a better, more empowering story.

Our brains will always seek to reinforce what we are focussed on, whether it's real or some story we are telling ourselves, so we might as well be consciously telling our selves stuff that empowers us and takes on the life path we want to follow. Changing your story takes a bit of upfront work, some practice at catching yourself when you default to old patterns. Fundamentally our brains like patterns, repetition, so the more you tell your new story the quicker it becomes your new default.

I believe as women of a certain age, we have unprecedented opportunities to make an impact, leave our footprint. I also believe we need the courage and the vision to step up, to move beyond our comfort zone and do what we really believe in.

So live or coast beyond 50, the choice is yours. I wish you success and happiness in your chosen path.

Lynda Holt developed Brave Scene, a community for ambitious business owners, as part of an award-winning international training and consultancy business. She has spent over 18 years working with thousands of business owners to shape, grow and evolve their businesses. Lynda has written a number of books on mindset, leadership and business development. Lynda's message is unequivocal: "show up, be brave and do what you believe in". Contact Lynda at www.lyndaholt.co.uk

STAINS ON HER SWEATER

A video shoot, create a root-toot,
Cause a stir, mustn't swear,
Judgement, vitriol, lurking there,
Amongst the common hoards.

Stains on her sweater?
Didn't you vet her? How could you let her?
How can we whet their appetites
when blighted by splurges of carelessness,
for all to see, a blot on her visibility?

Yet I yearn to caress her, bless her,
In all her authentic fragility, a stray wisp of hair,
Her eyes show she cares, so perfect
In all her vulnerability.

Sue Williams

Booba in Berkhamsted

Naomi Stevens

"Better late than never!"
— Naomi Stevens

I T WAS 1993. My father had been dead for three years. During that time, I'd had several similar conversations with my mother.
"Why don't you come and live with me and Nigel?"

"I'm fine on my own. I've got neighbours who not only look out for me, they are also friends." She named one of them who she said was more like a daughter to her than a friend. "She only lives on the floor below and sometimes she comes up here and other times I go down there. I'm OK."

Of course, I worried about her. Her fourth floor flat in central London was 30 miles away from our home in Berkhamsted. To get to see her we had a minimum of an hour's drive which could be worse depending on London traffic. What if the lift broke down and she had to walk up and down the stairs to go out and get back home?

She was adamant she would stay on her own until she had a fall. Fortunately, she was indoors, and her neighbour was with her, but it frightened her enough for her to agree to move in with me and Nigel.

It was coming up to her birthday, so we had a huge party for her to which all her friends and neighbours were invited. After everyone had left, we started the job of packing up the contents of nearly 40 years of living at 64 Shelley House. Trying to be methodical, I made lists and labelled boxes and large items and I booked a removal company. She actually moved in to our home the day after her 90th birthday.

After she'd settled in with us, we had to return the keys for her flat to the council. Nigel stayed at home while my mother and I made the journey together. Whilst we were out a friend visited Nigel and asked him where my mum and I were. Nigel's reply was accidentally priceless, "They've gone back to London to give back the fleas to the cat."

As a child I tried to please my mother but never felt I managed. No matter how good my school marks were or how well I did something, she always told me how it could have been improved. She never told me she loved me, never cuddled me except for Sunday mornings when I got into bed with her and my daddy.

I found out many years later that my father had once told her that fathers get left out, so she vowed that wouldn't happen to him. Instead of cuddling me herself, she'd tell him to give me a hug. I was eight years old the last time I had a cuddle of any sort during my childhood. It was a Sunday morning and as I climbed into bed with my parents, my father got up, put on his dressing gown and left the room. I didn't understand why. It didn't feel right just cuddling my mother, so I never got into their bed again. I didn't find out why this had happened until more than 45 years later.

My mum had been living with Nigel and I for several years when I decided to ask her questions about her childhood and record her answers. I'd made a list of things I wanted to know about, and she responded happily. Then she asked me to turn off the tape recorder. I did so and she told me that when she had been eight years old, she had been raped by a man who was such a regular visitor to their home that she called him uncle. That's when it made sense that when I turned eight, she didn't want my father to be in bed with me. I know she couldn't help herself, but I know that there wouldn't have been any danger of that happening to me by my lovely daddy.

Because of my relationship with my mother in my formative years, (she always believed she was right about everything) I vowed that when she lived in our home, she would have to live by rules set down by Nigel and me, not by her own as had always been the case. This sometimes resulted in tears and even tantrums when being told she couldn't have her own way. But most of the ten years she lived with us were fine. We had laughter as well as tears.

When she'd been here for a few years we were visited by my cousin Jack. As a child I'd stayed with his parents during summer holidays from school. He was 20 or more years older than me and had always treated me kindly. However, this visit was to advise me to put my mother into a home rather than have her live with us. He asked my mother, "Are you happy living in Berkhamsted?"

When she wanted to know why he asked, he replied, "Wouldn't you prefer to live with people your own age who have the same interests as you? I've heard of a brilliant residential home not far from here so Naomi and Nigel could still visit you."

My mother started to cry. "I don't want to live anywhere else. I'm happy here."

Jack looked at me. "Don't you think she'd be better off being with folk of her own age, being looked after by professional staff who can make sure she's ok?"

"No. I believe my home is the best place for her. She's happy here and we're happy to have her here. She's no trouble, well not much anyway," (I smiled at her as I said that) "so there's no reason for her to move anywhere else no matter how good it is. This is the best place for her."

During the remaining years my mother lived with us, we had extensive work done on our home so that she would have her bedroom and her own bathroom downstairs. (She was riddled with arthritis and it had been heart-breaking to listen to her struggling up the stairs where her original room was.)

Several years on I once asked her why she'd never told me she loved me. After that, she would occasionally say, "I love you." But then she'd add, "but I don't know why." I didn't really notice the add-on remark until one day Nigel said to me, "I love you and I do know why."

Coming up to my mum's 100th birthday I arranged for her to have a huge party. We'd booked a local pub and had decorated it, taking down huge amounts of food to feed all the family and friends who were coming. I'd contacted the palace to arrange the telegram from the Queen. This turned out to be a card with Her Majesty's picture on the front and her signature inside. Receiving that was a story all of its own. As was the party they made for her at the Day Centre she went to every week. My mother had loved watching Birds of a Feather on TV and Dorian was her favourite character. Lesley Joseph, the actress who played Dorian, is the cousin of a friend, so I'd managed to get her to come to her party to wish my mum happy birthday. Lesley was lovely and brought with her a cuddly teddy bear as a birthday present.

By now age was catching up with my mother. She now had the innocence of a young child, asking permission to watch TV or do some colouring. We'd print off blank pictures for her to colour then put the finished artwork on the wall where she could see it. Carers came to help her get washed and dressed in the mornings, whilst I helped her at night. Our evening routine was for her to sit on the side of her bath. I'd wash her face and her hands, then after I'd dried her, I'd put toothpaste onto the head of her electric toothbrush. As I handed it to her (she liked to brush her own teeth) I stood behind the sink so that when she turned the brush on, which she did BEFORE putting it into her mouth, I wouldn't get too many speckles of toothpaste on my shoes.

With her ablutions finished, we'd go into her bedroom. I'd rub moisturising cream onto her legs where the skin had got so fine it flaked away, then rub a different cream onto her arthritic joints to ease them. Once she'd been anointed in all the relevant places, I'd help her into her pyjamas. Our final ritual was for me to sit beside her on her bed where I'd put my arm round her to give her a night-time cuddle.

On the 30th June 2003, whilst helping my mum do her teeth, she looked up at me with one of her big, innocent, wide-eyed looks and asked, "Are you my daughter?"

When I replied that I was, she said, "I thought so."

Not long afterwards, when we had just started our regular nightly cuddle, she snuggled into me and said, "No wonder I love you so much. You're my daughter."

My mother died four weeks later on the 28th July 2003.

For everyone who is a carer for someone:

1. Be aware that your needs are just as important as those of the person you are caring for.

2. If your parent moves into your home, be prepared to establish your house rules. Don't let the past experience with the parent being the boss influence your decisions.

3. Be aware that having been brought up in a different generation they may not understand present-day ideas or concepts. Be mindful and maintain your own boundaries.

Naomi Stevens, a great-grandmother, lives in Berkhamsted with her husband Nigel. Now retired from teaching computer applications, Naomi practices and teaches Tarot and Astrology. She combines these subjects with her love of writing. She is in the process of publishing her Astrology book, which makes the subject simple for beginners. Find out more at: www.naomistevens.co.uk

OLD AGE

I hate old age
The very thought disgusts me
I run and fight with all my might
Because it's out to get me

Do not ask me to embrace it
I hate it
I want to be young
To have that youthful glow
I want to be admired you know

I want time to change my mind
To climb Mount Everest
Time to become a rock star
To write the book of books
To know exactly who I am

It's too soon to be old
I want to get undressed
Have sex
Not care
Be bold
Not old
Please let me

Elizabeth Beetham

Back to Your Future

Nicci Bonfanti

*"To be successful, the first thing to do is
fall in love with your work"*
— *Sister Mary Lauretta*

I N 2017, I had a flourishing coaching business with corporate clients, an Academy of regular private clients, a training school for teaching other coaches my methodology, online programmes accessible to all – everything a successful coach was supposed to have ... but I felt miserable, bored and unfulfilled.

Fast forward to 2018, and I am working in a completely different job, one that I love, that keeps me busy, active, thrilled and totally fulfilled.

What if you find yourself at a crossroads and know you need a change but don't know what it is?

Back in 2017 I knew something had to change. I wasn't motivated in my business and I was distracting myself by doing other things. I spoke to my mum about it. My mum has the advantage of having known me all my life and recognising when I'd been happiest in the past. She asked me what I'd wanted to do when I was younger

What did you want to be when you grew up? Take a moment to think about it.

In my case, after a brief period of wanting to be a long-distance lorry driver (influenced by the *Yorkie* adverts of the 1970's) my overriding ambition was to be a teacher and a mother. I'd planned it all out - have my children in the summer holidays, have time to learn as well as teach, be in a classroom of my own, plan the lessons.

It sounded great to me and, despite failing all my A levels the first time around, I eventually made it to study a degree in Media Studies, one of the first of its kind in the UK back in 1982. I loved every minute of it!

Once I'd completed that I returned to my original dream of becoming a teacher and did a teacher training certificate (PGCE) and that's when things started unravelling.

Teaching was hard! It was non-stop, all day every day, in front of students, being judged and scrutinised by them as well as by all the teachers and lecturers coming in to observe you. Also, at that time nobody taught Media Studies in school so instead of teaching what I'd studied and loved, I ended up teaching English, Sociology and History without having necessarily even an O level (the old-style GCSE) in those subjects.

After what was for me, a traumatic teaching practice in Birmingham during the time of race riots, and teacher strikes, I couldn't face being part of the conveyor belt of a school-university-teaching cycle ... so I ran away to Italy.

Milan was on one of the stops on my Euro-rail journey and I'd met some lovely Italians during a summer job teaching English to foreign students back in Birmingham. Little did I know that my future husband was one of those! I ended up staying in Italy for 6 years teaching English and then going on to a great job doing teacher training and sales for a publishing company.

That led to a brilliant career in sales and marketing taking me on numerous trips around Europe, Eastern Europe, Asia and America. 15 years went by as I climbed the promotional ladders in front of me. Always feeling a little bit of a fraud as I didn't always know what I was doing, but my decisions seemed as good as most people's and my career and salary flourished.

What I really wanted during this time was to become a mother, but fate had other plans for me - I didn't conceive my miracle child until I was 39. So, I had time to see the world and build up lots of work and management experience.

But when the momentous event of my daughter's birth arrived, I gave up my career. I was fortunate that I could do that and be supported in every way by my husband. That was a magical time of living in a baby-centred bubble. I had no idea nor wish to know anything about the world outside. I was besotted.

But as my daughter started venturing out to school, I started to revisit what I wanted to do with my life. It had to revolve around her. So, at 42 I became a serial entrepreneur, initially running an Italian language school for children, and then with adults and school clubs. Then I ran a sales and marketing coaching business helping other business owners with their sales. All very enjoyable and mostly lucrative, but I started to get bored and to be honest, a bit lonely working from home.

Not only was I getting uninterested; I thrive on variety, but as my daughter was growing up and the idea of her leaving home was dawning on me, the thought of running a business on my own from home was less appealing.

I was confused, a bit depressed, going through the menopause, and wondering what was next for me. A wise woman once said to me that on the other side of the menopause was wisdom. That then we'd stop pleasing others and realize what we REALLY wanted to do and find something that pleases ourselves.

So, I thought about that, I spoke to my mum and I wrote a journal regularly to try and listen to that voice inside me that knew what I really wanted. I observed what I got joy from doing, what I had the most energy for ... and what I had the least energy for and procrastinated over.

That is how I returned to my original childhood dream to become a teacher.

I noticed the things I loved doing at the time: writing training sessions for my Academy of coaches (teaching), giving talks at network meetings and conferences (teaching), helping my daughter prepare for her GCSEs (teaching). I enjoyed the tutoring of my daughter so much I was spending more time finding resources and planning lessons for her than I was on my own business!

In the autumn of 2017, my daughter and I were visiting all the local 6th form colleges looking for her right next step, and I realised that this was helping me formulate my next step too.

When I'd taken my degree in Media Studies over 30 years before it was not a subject taught in schools so I didn't really use it, despite absolutely loving it. Now colleges and schools that we were visiting, were teaching Media and Film studies at GCSE as well as at A level. It was mind blowing. The thought of teaching Media or Film all day filled me with enthusiasm.

When I talked to my mum about it, she said she and my dad always thought I should have been a teacher.

So, in October 2017, aged 54, I rang the Department of Education and asked what I'd have to do to retrain as a Media teacher. After a few questions, the answer was - you don't need to retrain, just apply for jobs.

That was quite a surprise! Although it was what I really wanted, I didn't feel prepared. So, I gave myself the goal of getting job-ready within a year and aimed to have a full-time Media Studies teaching job by September 2018. I informed my clients and closed down most of my business in December 2017.

When your goals are that clear and you are convinced it is the right path, the stars align and things can happen very quickly to make it work for you.

The Media Studies syllabus was changing so all Media Studies teachers were in a similar situation – having to learn the new set texts and theories. As a result, the Exam boards and the British Film Institute were running training courses on them, so I signed up for those.

I wanted to get used to teaching young people again so I signed up to tutoring websites. There I met some lovely students who improved their predicted results as a result of working with me. It also meant I got to know the syllabus really well.

The big challenge was going back into the classroom. I signed up to supply agencies so I could get classroom experience before I launched into my new career (and check it really was for me as I still had a few bad memories from my teaching practice in Birmingham). Best move ever. They are constantly on the look out to find you a position and I had a good selection of paid teaching work for the rest of the school year.

My first placement was in a very rough mixed school in south London for a week teaching Religious Education. It was literally a baptism of fire! The students were badly behaved towards the teachers, and towards each other. The other teachers didn't bother to learn my name as they had so many different supply teachers passing through. Some classes I wasn't allowed to be alone in the room with the students because of the high threat of violence.

But I persevered. By my third day I was congratulated on doing a great job. I asked how they knew and apparently the noise levels were monitored from the corridor, and it was noted that my classrooms at the end of the day were tidy and in order. I thought that criteria quite a low standard.

As most cover teachers will find, I had to oversee posters being made. My youngest class was year 7. The 11-year olds were asked to draw and write about a religious story they had seen a film about. My automatic thought was to put the best posters up on the bare classroom walls. Apparently, this was unheard of for a supply teacher to do in that school and I had teachers popping in to see if it was true! But more importantly, I had year 7's bringing their friends along to proudly show them their handiwork on the wall.

It was tough, it was scary, but so fulfilling too. I was sad to leave there in the end. And I knew. I knew that I had found my vocation. I had fallen in love with my work again. Teaching was something I was good at, that I enjoyed, that was important and fulfilling, and it would distract me when the time came for my daughter to leave home.

I was offered jobs teaching English, which I did as a supply teacher, but I still had my heart set on being a Media Studies teacher.

In July 2018, I found it. A wonderful all girls state school, in fact the school my daughter had just left, teaching Media Studies full-time with plans to grow the department. I am loving every minute of it.

I'm enthused, inspired, fascinated by the girls and fulfilled by seeing the light bulbs go off in their heads. I have fun putting creative lessons together and educating them about the world, not just their syllabus.

I'm no longer lonely. I am surrounded by like-minded caring people who are fun to be with.

I've fallen in love with my work, and although the 300 girls I teach each week won't take her place, the emptiness my daughter will leave behind when she leaves home won't be quite so huge.

Three tips for finding the right path for you

1. Speak to people that know you well. Talk about what you loved doing when you were younger, what you love doing now. There will be something there to build on.

2. Once you have an idea of what it is you want, dip your toe in the water. Do temporary work, shadow someone doing your dream job, talk to lots of people who already do it (and are enjoying it). That way you will know practically as well as emotionally that that is what you really want to do.

3. Keep a journal. I'm sure a lot of people have told you this, but there is no better way for finding that voice inside you that has all the answers. Find a way of journaling that works for you whether it is writing, speaking into a Dictaphone, drawing or doodling. Tap into that inner voice.

After training as a teacher and teaching English as a Foreign Language in Italy, **Nicci Bonfanti** began a long career in International Sales and Marketing travelling throughout Eastern Europe and Asia. Nicci gave up her career when her daughter was born and spent the next 7 years teaching Italian in her own school, Ciao Ciao. Then in 2010, Nicci used her MBA to set up her Sales Coaching business, Trusted Sales Dynamics. After 7 years of that (!) Nicci returned to her first love, teaching, and is now a full-time Media Studies teacher in a girl's secondary school in Surrey.

SUMMON YOUR VOICE

The microphone stands before me.
Beyond, stretching into space,
Rows of empty benches.
Each absorbs a trace
Of speeches past, momentous,
By every creed and race.
Dare I approach the podium,
Claim my rightful place?

At the back they'll hardly hear me,
Unless I project my voice.
Will the spoken word endear me
To the harshest critics present,
From whom others take their cue?
Foolhardy, will they fear me,
As with wit and words I turn the screw,
Squeeze their limited expectations,
Keeping them scared and small,
Pick them up and shake them,
Hold them rapt, in thrall?

Mine is the power,
The energy, the light.
My words they will devour,
Ecstatic with delight;
As long as I don't cower,
Tremulous with stage fright...

Sue Williams

Autumn Leaves are the Brightest

Patricia Bow

"When the wind of change blows,
some people build walls, others build windmills."
— *Chinese Proverb*

WE ARE ALL a work in progress. Hopes and dreams are to be treasured and not forgotten, but there is a danger of them remaining a distant glimmering vision, and so never in your real world. They may be something unrealistic and unattainable, but I've found since being in my 50s, I have changed my attitude and no longer simply hope that something in my life might change or improve.

People say, "there is always hope," but hope is always in the future; a guiding and comforting light. I should really try to take notice of what I am saying, as I am writing this from personal experience, and I don't always follow my own advice.

It has taken a while to get used to being in my 50s. I definitely started off as being in denial and wanting to cling onto my 40s. However, it has since evolved into a fundamental turning point in my life. The clock suddenly seems to tick louder even though time isn't passing any faster. Rather than a clockface, I prefer to think of it as a speedometer instead. To think of the 50s as reaching another speed limit, the need to speed up what you get out of life and that it should not be a time to hit the brakes and slow down.

I have found that this ominous decade has sharpened my assessment of what I am aiming for in life and allowed me to focus as much as possible, on getting closer to those goals. However, as I said earlier, I am not very good at following my own advice, and I have found it enlightening to have realised that, it is not that unusual to be that way.

Much of the time we are our own worst enemies in holding ourselves back from making our dreams a reality. I came across my chosen quote at the beginning of this year and it immediately resonated with me. Such a vivid and clear illustration of what I am trying to achieve. I am determined to use what life has given me so far to build the most fantastic 'windmill.'

I am not sure if it's a sign of getting older or that infamous fear of failure that, either consciously or sub-consciously, stops you from pushing yourself, like a weighty anchor holding you back. What baffles me is it still happens with the things that bring you enjoyment or that you want to do. It's almost like you dare yourself not to do it.

I find it varies from day to day and what mood I'm in. Suddenly the most trivial little tasks begin to raise their devilish heads and you find yourself completely distracted from what you should or want to be doing, polishing your shoes or cleaning something in the house that is really not urgent.

I don't mean to be hypocritical as I am very guilty of this frustrating procrastination, but at least I am aware of it, and slowly getting better at putting things into action. I think life has a knack of hurling curve balls and challenges if you are not doing what you should be doing or following the right path in life. I am at the stage of dealing with those, often living on the edge, but it does make you appreciate every little thing, and to be more alert to opportunities. I do still have to give myself a mental kick sometimes, but it is becoming more effective and I think I'm getting closer to finding the right path.

The last five years of my life have been very turbulent, with one challenge or obstacle followed by another. Entering my 50s was pretty trivial in the scheme of things. In fact, looking back on it, passing that milestone actually helped polarise my purpose in life and helped strengthen my identity.

Despite the struggles and uncertainties; having left a relationship before it dragged me down even more, moved back to this area, having health issues affecting my mobility and finding work, having to move home five times in as many years through no fault of my own, finding temporary work through my versatility and positivity and building my business in the background; I feel very appreciative of having come out the other side. I am at least in the process of coming out the other side, in a climbing out of a burrow, blinking in the light, not sure what will happen next way!

It has been quite a test to stay positive, and I do have the occasional deviation, but generally speaking, my situation makes me extra alert to opportunities. In many ways I feel I am lucky to be so adaptable and am constantly learning from working in new environments and meeting new people. Some friends say, "I don't know how you live like you do," but it's not a choice, I have simply been faced with situations in which I have had to make the best decision that was available at the time. I could write a lot more about my various challenges in recent years, but I don't want to introduce too much negativity, as the main objective of what I am writing is how a positive attitude is so important.

A good friend gave me a gift a couple of years ago, which was a paperweight-sized stone with the words: "The greatest success is being yourself" engraved on its smooth shiny surface. Simple, brief and so true. Why are some of the simplest things in life the hardest to find? I wish I knew, but it doesn't mean you have to give up on finding them. Life would be very dull if everything was easily attainable, there would be no sense of achievement or fulfilment and no aspiration. I am trying to find my true self. I hate to say 'trying' as that sounds like a get out clause, and I only say it because of that evil anchor I mentioned before, which I am doing my best to shake off. See, not 'trying' to do my best, so I am getting there!

I remember a long time ago, having to write an essay entitled "Youth is wasted on the young – discuss." I think that youth is life's stepping stone to becoming your true self. Or rather it should be, but so much gets in the way. Not to mention the self-doubt and lack of self-belief thrown into the mix that may be there for a multitude of reasons.

Growing older is an advantage. In that you have the wealth of life experience to call upon and to learn from; the bumps and knocks, the challenges, the highs, the lows and have formed your thoughts and emotions by the time you reach your 50s and beyond. You are then fully equipped to actually BE yourself and to enhance or become who you are meant to be in this world.

After all, through all the seasons, it is the autumn leaves that are the brightest, when trees shout their individuality in brazen colour. This is your place and time in this world. So, be proud that you have reached such an incredible, mature stage in your life, having lived enough to know enough. Build that windmill!

Exercises

1. Surprise yourself - What has surprised me is how much faith and encouragement I have received from people in the last few years. It has helped me have more faith in myself. You don't necessarily receive it from the people you would most like to, but it has come from complete strangers in some cases, and it has been a very pleasant surprise.

   Don't be scared to let your light shine, get around to doing what you've always wanted to do, even if it's a tiny thing. How could you involve others? Embrace the feedback you receive as a result. Even if it is negative, turn it into a positive; something to learn from, as it is likely to be constructive and will help you assess your abilities and how to exceed any limitations. Many limitations are self-imposed, and the chances are that you may not ever have been aware of this, if you hadn't put yourself out there.

   What surprised me was the unexpected encouragement I received when I sang at an open mic that I attend each week with some friends. I was 'just having a go' really, but the fact that I was taken seriously by others, really spurred me on to take myself seriously. Take a moment to think about what you would like to have a go at. Open mic has become a new direction in my life, something I am working at improving. I was amazed how much enjoyment I got out of getting up there, another surprise. How will you surprise yourself, what new experiences will you try?

2. Acceptance - Learn to accept that you can't always be good at everything you try. Don't feel a failure, be pleased that you gave it your best shot rather than wondering in later years 'what if.'

   Accept getting older but not being old. One thing I have found while being in my 50s, is that everyone seems obsessed with talking about getting old, talking about not being able to do this and that any more. It took me a while to get used to it, but I do not define myself by my age. I hate pigeonholes, we are all individuals and some people are too ready to restrict themselves unnecessarily, because they feel it is expected or appropriate for their age. I spent a while wrestling with the change of perception in myself and from the outside world. I didn't want to feel any different, I certainly didn't want to feel old. There are enough changes that happen that we can't control in our lives, so why self-impose even more. Think of one thing you would love to do yet haven't yet done because you think you are too old. Go and do it!

3. Be open - Be aware of what's around you. The smallest thing could spark off a thought that becomes an idea to inspire you, so take notice and let it grow. We are surrounded by opportunities all the time, some slip by or it's not the right time. The right time will present itself. For example, me having the opportunity to write this. I didn't seek it out, it came about in a very indirect way and I nearly ignored it. What I've written has been bubbling away in my mind for a while, so I welcomed the opportunity to express my thoughts and share them. It was the right time. Take note when something seems significant or strikes a chord, and perhaps carry a notebook and pen with you so you don't let opportunities slip by un recorded.

Patricia Bow has over twenty years of experience in communications, copywriting, design, marketing and events related projects in a variety of sectors. Her balance of creative and lateral thinking, combined with strong organisation and planning abilities enable her offer new perspectives to pinpoint and inspire new direction and opportunities. Most of Patricia's current clients are connected with health, wellbeing, leisure or relaxation under the brand name of Basking Lizard which is also being developed into a collaborative website. You can find Patricia on Linked In.

WINDS OF CHANGE

Tender rain
Caress my pain,
As I walk and think alone.

Moody cloud
So quiet and proud,
Shadow my solitude.

Stirring breeze
Untamed and free,
Whisper the turmoil in my soul.

Patricia Bow

Money Healing for the Soul

Rosemary Cunningham

"Money isn't everything
but it ranks right up there with oxygen".
— Zig Ziglar

BECAME A MONEY mindset coach, seemingly by accident, in 2010!
I was 46, my sister had just died of cancer. In considerable debt, I
was unable to pay it off with the earnings from my complementary
therapy business. As I had just hit the menopause, my chances of
having the family I longed for had passed. Life was nudging me on my
path in a huge way. Although I resisted for years, finally taking the leap
and using the last £495 on my credit card to book the Money Coach
training truly shaped my life going forward. It has enabled me to make
the biggest difference yet. I still feel thrilled that I made that decision
and invested in myself.

Back then, I was a full-time complementary therapist. I had been
running my own busy practice from my home since 1993. I loved my
work and my clients but I had accumulated debt and wanted to find an
alternative source of income.

I never expected to be single, childless and living by myself at 46.
That just wasn't my life plan at all.

I had set up my complementary therapy practice, fully expecting
(hoping) that soon I would be running a part-time business around the

husband I was yet to meet, and children. To prepare for this eventuality, I trained in all sorts of child-related therapies – baby massage, baby reflexology and the Bowen therapy for children. I specialised in giving maternity treatments and helped many, many women have a great pregnancy. I also helped couples who had challenges with fertility to have babies.

However, despite nearly a decade of internet dating, I didn't meet a man to spend the rest of my life with. Having a child on my own just wasn't on my agenda.

When my sister Heather died of breast cancer, I recognised myself so much in her. She was a year older than me. This deeply unhappy, dissatisfied soul was a reflection of me in many ways. So, when she died, I was determined to get on with my life, have more fun and spend less time looking in the rear-view mirror. I abandoned the internet dating that obviously wasn't working and instead focused on my business, to give me the freedom I wanted.

I had accumulated a lot of debt which was stopping me just running away and playing, so I started researching the mindset it took to make money.

A course to train as a money coach for women miraculously jumped up on an internet search and I didn't over think that decision! Using my last £495 I made the first payment and signed up.

In my life, there have been a few pivotal "homecoming" moments. The first was when I became a student nurse, another was taking my first holistic massage course: Discovering Gentle Touch Reflexology with an amazing woman called Pat Morrell, and studying the Money Breakthrough Method was another.

I became hooked during the first money coaching session. I remember it so well. I was on a sunbed, under a parasol on a beach in Cyprus, having manifested a free holiday in a five-star hotel. I knew instantly this money stuff was something special, a different type of healing, healing for the soul and spirit. Excitement filled my body and a big smile crossed my face. That hadn't happened for some while.

In my heart, I sensed this approach was powerful and could really transform lives, starting with my own.

The course took a few months to complete and focusing on my relationship with money really brought up all my, what I call "money stuff". I hit rock bottom financially to a point where I was scared to open my bank account.

We had been assigned a buddy for the course. Mine was Martina, a wonderful woman, 20 years younger than me who kindly helped me. She suggested that I held a ceremony before I ventured into my bank account. I lit a candle, said a prayer, breathed - and I did it! I worked through my own money mindset, the beliefs about money that I had inherited from my family, and I tidied up my finances. This process was huge, as I had long been in chaos and denial. Up till now, I had no idea where my money was going but within a few weeks, the lights were well and truly switched on.

I qualified and embarked on an exciting new path as a Money Coach. The universe wanted me to use my voice more, not just my hands, and I had listened. The next phase of Rosemary's life was born. Life wanted to me to move forward. Eczema on my hands has meant that it is no longer possible to see as many therapy clients, so gradually the coaching has taken over.

I've fought it all the way though! Hands on therapy work was my comfort zone and I genuinely didn't feel successful enough, knowledgeable enough, anything enough to be helping other people with their money mindset and running their own businesses.

I also didn't feel successful enough myself to ask for the kind of money my mentor told me I should be charging.

I had enough trouble asking for the £45 an hour I charged for therapy treatments at the time, so how could I add a zero or two to that for a programme; asking clients for the kind of money I was paying for coaching? It was terrifying. Who would people think I was to be asking for the kind of money? The self-talk and old beliefs about money and what I deserved resurfaced, enormous and loud!

I was interviewed by the lovely Suzy Walker, now editor of Psychologies Magazine. Suzy was my first coach and she believed in me many years before I believed in myself – always the mark of a great coach.

From that interview alone, I got eight money coaching clients and I was paid more money in a week than I had ever earned in a month before.

That week I woke up in the middle of the night in a panic and cold sweat, terrified about where the next money was going to come from. That was an unforgettable money coach lesson, since repeated when I have come into large sums of money.

I knew there was something missing, I had more money healing to do. I started to work on my beliefs every day, making my own healing, money healing and building my business my biggest priority.

I felt I needed to learn more, that I wasn't good enough yet. So, I did more training, visiting Arizona six times in eighteen months to work with my mentor, Kendall Summerhawk, but still something was missing.

I continued to invest in myself, terrified that my business would fail. I borrowed huge amounts of money from my father to invest in coaching, buying the guidance of "intuitive" and financially successful coaches who I hoped would give me the confidence to achieve as much as they were. It was disastrous, I felt I was standing on a cliff edge.

The big turnaround came through gradually learning to access my own intuition, so I didn't have to pay someone else for theirs! One of my biggest lessons has been to find quiet in my life to discover how to access my heart energy.

If you want to try this, first take your attention right into the middle of your head. Imagine there's a tiny elevator or lift and take a mini you into the lift. Watch the doors close and press the button that says "heart space". Then feel the elevator drop deep, deep down inside you until it stops, around the base of your shoulder blades. Allow the lift doors to open and the tiny you to come out, into the peace and quiet of your own "Heart space". There, in the deepest, most sacred part of you, be quiet and visit often. There you can ask your questions and find your guidance, away from the busy-ness of your head.

I still grapple with my own "imposter syndrome" when it asks me once again who am I to do this? However, I've learnt to be kind to that part of me, my scared little five-year-old Rosemary who learnt that life can be very disappointing, money has to be struggled for and success has to be hard earnt and fought for. My big Rosemary believes in living peacefully with grace and ease, being happy in my own skin, sharing what I love and then life and business come with joy and ease. It's a work in progress but more of my reality each and every day.

Business is the biggest change agent that we have. We are changing the world through heart-centred business. That feels a little ostentatious to write, but I genuinely believe it's true. I feel that my higher self has created this reality so I can do what I came here to do, which is to help womankind step into their true role in the world, helping the planet to move forward as a caring, sharing place. To help fulfill this desire, I started Winning Women Essex a supportive, business networking community. This has helped both me and hundreds of other women to have the independence they want through running their own businesses, whether tiny or big!

Business, life and money are 90% about your mindset, 10% about action. So, give your mindset and your little girl or boy some attention and keep going back to it. We are all a work in progress, and if you're on a path, you're constantly learning about yourself. Prioritising your own development is crucial and ongoing.

So, my advice is, take a look at your mindset about money. How we do money is how we do everything. Learning about you and money beliefs and habits is hugely valuable for everyone and will pay you back many times over.

To your happiness and success with grace and ease!

Three exercises.

1. Ask yourself, what did/do my mother and father think about money? If you didn't know your parents, substitute the dominant adults (church, teachers, grandparents etc.) who were in your life up to the age of 7 years old. Journal what you were hearing and seeing, the sayings and how you felt about them. Think about how these have manifested in your life to date.

2. Monitor your spending for a month. Write down absolutely every-thing that you spend, every penny. Add the columns up and see where your money really is going. This awareness alone, is priceless.

3. How would you treat money if it was holy? If money were really special and sacred to you, how would you treat it? Would you treat it with respect, save more, be really careful what you did with it? Look at your cash, the notes and coins that make up money are really beautiful and full of symbolism. Get to know and enjoy them. Use cash wherever possible so you really feel your money and appreciate it.

Rosemary Cunningham is a Money, Marketing and Soul Coach and believes that business is our most powerful vehicle for world change. Her passion is changing the world through heart-centred business. Rosemary helps women to move from struggle to independence and empowerment, attract their ideal clients and make great money doing what they love!

Rosemary ran her own busy complementary therapy practice in Essex for over twenty years, helping thousands of clients of all ages with challenges from fertility issues to chronic pain. More recently, she founded Winning Women Essex, a supportive community for women in business.

Find out more at: www.rosemarycunningham.co.uk.

I REACHED THE AGE OF FIFTY PLUS

I reached the age of fifty plus,
Still feeling an awkward wuss.
Carried careless playground scorn;
Worked many years,
Playing out my fears
In a job that made me yawn!

I crossed a chasm,
Felt like a spasm,
That propelled me towards life.
Yet despite some play,
Creativity, along the way;
The past cut into me like a knife.

So how to break loose
From this papoose;
So tightly clawing at freedom?
Untie the strings that bind me in,
And release my inner wisdom?
I'll write a book,
With a powerful hook;
Full of wonderful wit and words.
So, if advice is took
By those who look,
They'll rise above the starving herds
Of cattle, huddled close for comfort.

Strip back the fear, the shiny veneer,
That keeps them warm and safe;
Unleash the passion buried within
That at their hearts does chafe.

Sue Williams

Believe in Your Uniqueness

Sue Williams

"Beauty begins the moment you decide to be yourself."
— *Coco Chanel*

MY LIPS TWITCH into a wry smile. How ironic that I have chosen to start this story with a quote from Coco Chanel, the originator of the legendary "little black dress". One thing I knew for certain from a fairly early age was that I disliked black clothes. It seemed strange that so many people would choose to wear clothes in this particular shade. Wearing black left my face looking pale, drained of life. Yet, a proliferation of black dresses, trousers, coats and scarves adorned clothes rails throughout my late teenage years.

Of course, there are advantages of wearing black, even when it isn't the most suited of colours. Black trousers can do wonders for a full figure, and wearing a lovely warm coloured blouse cancels out the wan, washed out effect. And, of course, when black does actually form part of a woman's own colour palette, suiting her personal skin colouring, it does look absolutely stunning!

As a teenager, though, I much preferred to wear navy. Navy, and various other shades of blue. I also had a penchant for purple. I recall a particularly loved pair of lilac, flared trousers. And yes, I also preferred to wear trousers to dresses. This at a time when many employers still had rules that forbade women from wearing trousers to work.

Choosing navy coloured clothes for leisure wear might seem a pretty conventional choice. After all, we are talking a deep shade of blue here, not bright orange or yellow, brilliant red or clashing stripes. However, the regulation school uniform at the girls' grammar school I attended was navy and white. So, when my mother took me shopping to buy clothes, she would protest when my natural inclination was to buy additional navy or blue items. "You wear navy for school, already. You should go for something different when you are at home," she would protest. "How about this?" She would select something that appealed to her from the rail, and I would dutifully try it on, my heart sinking as my desired garment was unceremoniously returned to the rail.

There it is. Did you notice it? Buried within a simple sentence on an everyday shopping trip. A seemingly innocuous word. Yet one that causes mayhem with our self-belief and sense of self-worth. I refer to that most insidious of over-used words; "should." By the time we reach our fifties, we have experienced a whole tsunami of "shoulds." No wonder we can be left feeling that our sense of self is not at all strong.

Perhaps you relate? Over the years it has become second nature for a sea of shoulds to wash over us. We "should" do as we are told, "should" try harder, "should" tidy our bedroom, "should" do well at school, "should" meet a suitable partner... "should" settle down and have a family, "should strive for promotion" "should be the strong one" ... You know the drill! Yet often, after doing what we should, we end up feeling less sure of ourselves, not more confident of who we are meant to be.

Those pesky "shoulds" are particularly damaging when coupled with comparisons – implied or otherwise.

"Why can't you be more like your cousin Carole?" my mum would say in exasperated tones when once again I failed to match up with her ideal of what a daughter should be like. Had I been more self-aware, the obvious retort would have been along the lines of, "because I am nothing like Carole, I am me. We are totally different people, with totally different colouring, looks, abilities and interests." Instead, unseen under a bob of mousey brown hair, a never-ending spiral of unanswerable "whys" whirled around my brain. Blonde, capable Carole continued her seemingly gilded existence, oblivious that she was being lauded as a perfect feminine role model to which I would never match up. To whom, I now belatedly realise, I was never meant to match up.

With the benefit of hindsight, it is strangely fascinating, and deeply disturbing to consider how seemingly casual references can blight our lives for decades. Unchallenged, limiting beliefs take root, and worry their way through our psyche like burgeoning weeds choking back a nascent flower. No wonder by the time we reach our fifties many of us find ourselves operating on autopilot, doing what we have always done, struggling with a sense that "there must be more to life than this", yet baffled about where to start and how to make clear decisions around what is truly best for us.

Certainly, on reaching the age of 51, after deciding to take a tempting offer of early retirement from work, I suddenly realised that I had no idea who I was or what I wanted to do with my life. You see, I had been working for the civil service in a role that was increasingly unsatisfying due to changing government policy and budget cuts. Over the years, a creeping sense of feeling dull and lacklustre permeated my being. Fading into the background, I felt like an insignificant grey blob on tired, stained wallpaper. Admittedly, the small team of which I was a part assured me that they appreciated my calming presence, always the "peace keeper" amongst strong personalities. Yet I felt powerless, with no voice.

I have already indicated how much I like blue. For those readers versed in the chakras, you will already recognise blue as relating to the throat chakra. It represents communication. Increasingly over my 51-year life span, I allowed myself to lose sight of my own voice. Lacking the confidence to pursue a career in journalism in my teens, I habitually sought to conform, to fit in.

Pinging into our inboxes one day, the email announcing the enticement of early retirement/voluntary severance was met with a hub bub of chatter. Some feared for their job security and salary, others, like me felt their spirits lift at the offer of a pay-out and a pension. An opportunity to escape the constant stop, start, stop, start nature of the changing working environment.

Despite dissenting voices enquiring "what will you do with yourself if you leave?" "Won't you miss having a job?" or the odd incredulous – "you must be mad!" I was definite that this was time to go. Staying was too terrible an option to contemplate – one day I might just slide under my desk and disappear completely through a crack in the lino. What was more, my mother was terminally ill. Following the unexpected death of my dad a year earlier, she had almost immediately been diagnosed with cancer. I was commuting to Leicester from Coventry to visit her in her care home as often as I could.

A woman of strong opinions, I had spent my life trying to please mum. I take comfort from the fact that, in her final months, she genuinely appreciated my support. Maybe she finally realised I was a person in my own right with my own positive qualities, rather than someone through whom she attempted to live her own thwarted dreams. Don't get me wrong, I admired my mum, and as an intuitive sensitive related strongly to how she had been hampered by society's expectations leading her to leave work on having her first child and believing that a woman's place is in the home. Thank you, mum, for doing your best for us when it was so hard for you to do your best for you.

After mum died, a new year dawned in which two constants in my life – my parents and steady employment, were no longer present. Suddenly, it hit me. I had no idea who I was or what I wanted to do with my life. On the spur of the moment, I signed up for a free two-day coaching course, sparking a journey of exploration. That first evening I felt more alive than I could remember, due to experiencing the obvious enthusiasm of two trainers openly doing what they loved, coupled with the energy and excitement of the entrepreneurial world. Unwittingly, I became a "course junkie."

As with most journeys, there were many ups and downs, and detours along the way. Writing poetry was one unexpected avenue that opened up to me. Having started writing Morning Pages, a journaling technique taken from a book, *The Artists Way*, my writing spontaneously emerged in rhyme. Poetry became a means for expressing myself, exploring my buried emotions and confronting my deep-rooted lack of self-belief. Concurrently, I discovered a passionate enthusiasm for the world of self-publishing. Having encountered disheartened people who had quashed their dreams of writing a book after a series of rejection letters, the self-publishing route seemed to offer a beacon of hope and opportunity to aspiring authors. I felt drawn to publishing a book of my own.

Could I really do it? Where would I start?

The answer arrived swiftly - in a poem! Not just any poem, but one called Believe! that I had penned myself. This wake-up call in rhyme flowed from my pen one morning in response to the theme -Believe in Your Dreams, Your Legacy, Your Power - of an event a friend was planning. Around three months later, I rediscovered the Believe poem on my computer. Realisation dawned as I re-read my words, words that reflected my experience of feeling squashed and ignored, of finding my own voice strangled.

Immediately I thought "I am meant to do this! I am meant to publish a book!"

I set a goal to write and collate true stories on the topic of self-belief. It seemed natural to capitalise on my networking activities and inherent energy as a connector. Why not gather stories from the inspirational entrepreneurial women I was meeting? Entering a challenge to write a Kindle book spurred me on, and I was bolstered by the support and encouragement of friends and women I met. Fittingly, an artist in a spiritual group to which I belonged produced a beautiful drawing of a rainbow, arching over the word Believe which provided the inspiration for the cover.

How apt – the vibrant, multi coloured image encapsulated the strength and diversity of the different women contributing to the book. After all, whilst the pages of books are generally black and white, the essence of their contents so rarely are.

My self-belief has grown incrementally during my fifties, and I continue on the journey to develop my voice. I am naturally one of the "quiet ones" who loves to support and promote others. Yet, on reaching my sixtieth birthday, I am the proud publisher of 4 books, including my own poetry book, *I Am Unique* which became a best-seller by knocking none other than Jane Austen off the top spot in its category on Amazon! I also went on to create the award-winning Believe oracle cards. The cards, like my book covers, are emblazoned with colour.

We all have the ability to paint our own vivid picture that illuminates our dreams, bolsters our inner sense of power and self-worth, and creates our own beautiful contribution to this multi-coloured world. Mine of course, will possess significant quantities of blue and purple.

Exercises

1. Be aware of the language that you are using. When you find yourself saying "I should" or "I ought" make a note in your journal. For example, "I should go and visit mum" or "I ought to go to the gym". Ask yourself how often you use these phrases. You might also want to jot down other things you notice, such as when you say "yes" when you really want to say no.

2. Study the examples above in more depth. Ask yourself – do I really want to do this? If the answer is no, dig a little deeper – where is this "should" or "ought," coming from? Does your mum put pressure on you to visit? Have you signed up for the gym and feel you ought to go because you are spending so much money, or because your friends want you to join them? Now make some decisions. When you really want to do something, start using language such as "I choose to…", or "I enjoy exercising". Notice what difference this makes in your day to day life.

3. How can you bring more colour into your life? You may want to experiment with wearing different colours. What colours lift your mood? What colours do you resist and why? Create a mood board of the colours that reflect how you want to feel and the things you want to achieve in your life.

Sue Williams is an author and poet, and creator of the *Believe You Can* series of inspirational books for women. She won a Gold award in 2017 for her inspirational Believe Oracle Cards app, and achieved top spot in her category on Amazon on release of *I Am Unique*, her first poetry book. Sue holds events for women to help them claim the power of their own signature success stories. Find out more at www. sue-williams.com

ALL ABOUT THE BOY

Dumbed down, deadened down,
Sit in silence, feel a clown.
Cry less, be more,
Open wound, weeping sore,
Barbie girl that all adore.
Silent, plastic, nothing more.

Made of elastic, expand and grow,
Let them know you can knit and sew,
Sing, cook, play piano; looks always in place,
Synthetic smile plastered on your face.

Lace hankies, chair covers,
In bed at night, static lovers.
True self, reality smothers.

No mind of your own,
A worthless clone,
A procreator, incubator,
He's off to the pub, "See you later".

Riddled with guilt and self-doubt,
Dutiful role, flawlessly plays out,
Deeply inbred, you cannot flout;
Silenced; urge to scream and shout.

Forever condemned to suppress your joy;
History proclaimed "It's all about the boy".

Sue Williams

Transformation

Susan Nefzger

*"Do not go where the path may lead, go instead where there
is no path and leave a trail."*
— *Ralph Waldo Emerson*

EXPERIENCES CHANGE OUR lives and transform our inner being. The
energy created by this process allows us to make the choices that
move us to the next step on the path. Have you ever realised that
your entire life is changing in the moment as you observe it? That was
the effect that writing through inspiration had on my life in May of
2015.

Transformation via the creative consciousness…and what a journey
it has been!

It all began with a feeling of synchronicity surrounding the energy
associated with an email regarding a writing retreat in Glastonbury,
England. I felt a magnetic pull so strong that I decided to attend
the conference as I had been ruminating over writing a book. So, I
travelled from the U.S. to London, then to Somerset, Glastonbury.
What began as a feeling, a clue, an intuition - ended up as a reunion of
souls; of people with which a common feeling of sisterhood pervaded
our energy, conversations and activity.

Flashback to my journey of self-realisation during the thirty
years prior - working as a successful public relations executive mainly

through my own business. But since the days of being on the Georgia Lottery start up team, living in Atlanta, I had a feeling that I was missing something. I literally had my epiphany in those years with many soulmates assisting me.

Earlier on I read "Many Lives, Many Masters" by Brian Weiss M.D. in the 1980's, and the lightbulb switched on to the clues surrounding our soul and its significance in the life of our human inter -workings. Attending his workshop on past lives and studying other masters, and in particular following Paramahansa Yogananda and the Self-Realization Fellowship, I was on a quest to figure out my purpose. I had always wanted to write a book, but I never quite felt the burning motivation that I experienced after my trip to Glastonbury.

From the moment I arrived there I was ensconced in pure light, love and spiritual memories that transported me to another time and place. Thus, inspiration began as I crafted lines from another century and another perspective. The meaning was unclear. I followed the trail of clues that was something indefinable. This began for me a new life of writing and being in alignment with my true purpose. Little did I know at the time, this realignment would take over my daily activity and literally change my entire life, from head to toe, including my business and my relationships.

I went on the trip to the UK without expectations but knowing it was meant to be. I did know that age 54 I was sure there had to be something more for me, but it was not anything I could define then. I led a settled life, yet the mystery would be revealed as I agreed to the journey.

I began writing my book entitled, "A Practical Guide to Awareness" on the very first day of the gathering. I wrote it in six weeks, and I employed a professional editor to assist me in the publishing process. That drafting and editing process took a bit longer, as I was still working, my husband was opening a restaurant and my son was getting ready to graduate from high school. Did I need to be self-aware and present during all of these life changing experiences? Yes.

Apparently, the path led to that discernment of self-exploration over a couple of years of trial and tribulation. But I never gave up on the process because I knew that this was my true calling to share with the world. I learned that in supporting everyone else in their dreams, I had left mine behind. But the universe took me and dropped me into the world of spiritual writing to remind me that I did, indeed, have a special purpose. We all do have a gift to share with the world. That is the detective work for all of us!

The breadcrumbs on the path and the inspiration led me to rework my business model. I was running my own consultancy, and I recognised that I wanted to work with people who were helping others. So, I changed my work focus which led to less income. I was also writing the book, editing it and beginning to write poetry. What a mystery that presented! I just went with it and first published my poetry blog "Seeing Beyond the Ordinary - Discover the Beauty in Each Day" on WordPress during this time. It felt so fulfilling. The blog page encompasses both my poetry and photography.

A new mystery was revealed as I had never written poetry before in my life. What a surprise that it came pouring out of me at every inspirational turn! I was perplexed. The tap, tap, tap on my shoulder each morning could not be ignored as the words and visions for my book were channelled into my mind and I relayed them as best I could through the written word onto the page.

Fitting in time to get it all down on paper was a challenge. I wrote each morning, waking early enough to have quiet time to myself. Having completed the initial writing, I began editing and was introduced to an editor through an old friend. Synchronicity occurred every step of the way in this lovely process of trusting in my divine gift and remaining in alignment. The process has been mind-boggling and wonderful; but it was not easy at all.

During this time, my business suffered, as I had changed the thrust of what I was doing and who I was working with, based on my need to stay in alignment with my true path. My husband's restaurant took up all of his time and energy. Sadly, as I felt I must, in order to remain true to myself, we divorced because of the differences that became apparent in our values and ethics surrounding work and money. That was a shock to me, but one I have gradually grown accustomed to and moved on from after following clues and listening to my intuition.

Also, it must be said I have always had a strong faith in the Creator or Collective Consciousness, which is my inner strength and serves as my "detective" of sorts. Does it feel right, does it feel good and is it for the greater good? These are all questions I ask myself when making decisions.

In solution or resolution for women over age 50 who have been married, had kids, attained a degree of career success but still feel unfulfilled, trust that it may just be the beginning! That is the premise of my book, becoming self-aware in order to discover your true gift.

I know that something better is in store for me as I continue the journey of publishing and promoting the information in my book for the world to access. Maybe I needed to do that on my own, without the stress and pull of a partnership in love. I believe it is all happening for a reason. I believe that each of us shall lift up the planet with the discovery of our true gift.

I am beginning to do more writing for a living, including ghost-writing. These changes are ever present and fluid, as are other new dimensions. As I ponder this story, I cannot believe the changes that have occurred in my life and it all started with Conscious Writing which follows a distinct process to become aligned with your creative consciousness.

I recommend that you explore the three exercises that have enabled me to do all of this in the last two years for yourself:

1. Engage with a daily Conscious Writing morning practice. Or any daily morning process of writing and quiet time. My morning practice consists of a breathing and connecting exercise that grounds your energy and aligns you with creative consciousness. I have found that it helps me set an intention for the day and stay in the aligned energy of that initial morning moment.

2. Write daily. It can be a short poem, or an idea, or a part of whatever you are creating. For me, it can be writing a few words that come

to mind, or accessing my book to find a quote to share on social media. This aligns me to my path through the energy of the book.

3. Walk outside and photograph nature. Without my writing and photography, I would not be here. What this exercise does is to make you present and notice everything that comes your way. Hence, my poetry blog, "Seeing Beyond the Ordinary- Discover the Beauty in Each Day." I believe that if we can see the everyday beauty surrounding us then we can be inspired to create paradise on earth. This is what I attempt to share with everyone through my photographs and poetry; to uplift people on this journey called life and help people discover their true purpose through self-awareness.

Susan Nefzger resides in Atlanta, Georgia. She has explored self-awareness since the early '80's after reading "Many Lives, Many Masters," by Brian Weiss, M.D. Whilst a member of the Georgia Lottery start-up team, she began a self-actualisation quest. During a substantive 30-year career in public relations, Susan travelled the world seeking answers. At a retreat in Glastonbury, UK in 2015, a torrent of inspiration flowed which became her book, "A Practical Guide to Awareness", and its companion "Putting Awareness into Practice." Susan's blog, "Seeing Beyond the Ordinary" combines her poetry and nature photography. Susan also offers online courses and workshops. For more information, visit: http://snefzgerpr.wordpress.com

A BLANK PAGE

Faced with a blank page, my future, my life,
Staring back at me, taunting me, I stall at the enormity
Of this clarion call for creation. Hesitant mark appeared,
Blemishes pristine whiteness. Or a blessing? Venture
Forth, unleash meaning and mission, magnificence and joy.
The embodiment of all that I am, all that I can be,
Committed to paper, for all to see.

Or cowardly, baulk at this honour?
The ultimate power to create a flamboyant future,
Shine beaconlike; showcase my very essence.
Sweep through swathes of darkness,
With irrevocable light.

Beauty of life, teaming possibility,
Swimming with the tide; in flow.
Thoughts, words and deeds undulate.
Soul expression in motion,
Surging tumultuously into life.

Sue Williams

A Life Most Ordinary

Sylvi Hussain

I'm nobody! Who are you?
Are you nobody, too?
Then there's a pair of us -- don't tell!
They'd banish -- you know!
— Emily Dickinson

'VE BEEN ASKED to write about my story - a life changing, road to Damascus moment; Light, Clarity, Purpose all in one flash! Although, for me, it didn't happen in quite such an apocalyptical manner; it came to me quietly and grew as does the best love per Mama Cass.

This is a celebration of the quiet life, the ordinary life, the ordinary happenings and occurrences which nevertheless lead to extraordinary shifts, transformations and richness beyond measure.

An ordinary life, which I deliberately curated. Growing up, in my world, everything was extraordinary: my parents, my background, the people who gravitated towards my family, my ethnicity, my name (in a world where the phrase 'ethnic minority' and all its connotations had not yet been coined) was extraordinary… in that I stuck out like a sore thumb. I didn't like it …

And thereafter all my endeavours were directed to be the Ordinary.

I hankered after anonymity; not to have to answer the question-where are you from, not even where is your family from? How do you say your name? Why do you speak with an English accent?

My world picture was cosmopolitan white. I was not quite a born but certainly a bred, north London child, having moved gradually north from Golders Green via Temple Fortune to North Finchley.

We then moved right out to Watford in the late 60's and boy was that a culture shock- yes I wanted to retreat to ordinariness, and walk close to the wall, because the alternative was the racism and misogyny which lived in these outer areas, better documented by others.

Retreat into ordinariness seemed to be the order of the day!

Time went on - I desperately wanted to fit in, or so I thought. What I actually wanted was not to be quizzed, and to be just accepted without having to explain myself. I wanted to be in a place where every-one knew how to say my name, and there wouldn't be the same repetitive questions, and I could be without fear.

So, Reader, I did it through marriage! I married him, went to live in Pakistan to lead a life most ordinary; to be liked, for assumptions to be positive ones, to blend in. But no - extraordinariness hounded me. I was English speaking, didn't really get the hang of the reality of the local culture; my husband and in-laws were extraordinary and wanted to be more so...I just wanted a quiet blending in life. What's wrong with that I want to know? I certainly didn't want to be extraordinary to order.

There was a mismatch there and clearly a difference in aspiration; alas, Reader, as I married him, so I left him, or rather I prefer to use the narrative of he left me!

I came back HOME to England with my 2-year-old precious daughter and set to constructing A Life Most Ordinary.

Starting work with a Local Authority, in what I thought was a very ordinary role, I worked up to managerial level, whilst I brought my daughter up. The irony is I wanted **her** to be extra-ordinary in all the right ways

Evidently, secretly I do value the extra-ordinary and truth be told all that I did was extra-ordinary. I brought my daughter up, whilst dealing with a narcissistic mother and forged my seemingly ordinary career. I managed to remain in the same organisation for more than 25 years. My daughter grew up and has forged an extraordinary career as a city lawyer.

My humdrum life continued until .... drumroll, I met someone! Yay! I was to be humdrum no more, if I was to be extraordinary, I could do it with someone else - and there lies the rub: I was afraid of standing out on my own - scared of being seen, scared of ridicule, scared of being exposed, scared of failure, scared of being asked to do stuff, taking on responsibilities that I wouldn't or couldn't fulfil – Scared. But with ANOTHER, I could: I could be seen either in the light or shadow of someone else. I wouldn't be solely responsible I would be able to share.

As with most organisations, whether in the public or private sectors, the dreaded word 'reorganisation' was being bandied about. With sheer hutzpah or complacency, I ignored it.

Pah, I thought, I had my chap, I had been there for so long, what could possibly go wrong?

Well, Reader, wrong it did go, with a crash, bang and a jolly old wallop!

My relationship floundered, burnt and crashed - for the most common of reasons: he wanted to go back to his previous paramour - I was as crushed and deflated and hurt and humiliated as any 17-year-old. I wanted ordinary - I got ordinary and common!

To add insult to this humiliating injury, my role was indeed made redundant. I endured a painful interview with my manager where the word redundant was actually uttered to me, about me, in the cold light of day and with cold breath. I had never actually heard the expression in reality and in relation to me - thus far it had been a mere abstraction, heard on the news, known of other departments and hapless colleagues. Like death, I never thought it would happen to me.

Let me just dwell on this for a moment: death, redundancy, divorce/separation, evictions. All final; endings. To experience these events is very different to hearing about them, imagining, sympathising, empathising; the private thought is - it won't happen to me.

But, dear heart, it does, and it will! And when it does, it doesn't put a comforting arm round your shoulder, it does not utter whispered words of wisdom, it does not offer the warm space of an alternative, it does not proffer a sustaining drink.... it is cold, hard, unyielding in its truth, and tests you as it thinks a grown-up should be treated. The blow is delivered without flinching and you take it, internally crouched, but on the chin, pretending it's not wobbling.

It leaves you feeling bereft, floored, weak, cold.

At least that is the effect it had on me. This coming hard on the heels of the break-up - rejection as I chose to see it at the time.

I took a few days off work to 'compose myself' and collect my thoughts. Wandering round the local shopping mall in a daze, the thoughts started to form themselves, with the vocabulary of worthlessness, rejection, defeat, misery, despair. I was not new to this: the last time I had been assaulted on all fronts was when my marriage broke up, no husband, no job, no home - because he wanted to be with some-one else. How banal?

I didn't go into free fall then because I had my daughter for whom I had to rise and be strong, provide sustenance, a roof, education, - everything that parents do for their children. I could not afford to crumble into a heap. At that time, I shed a few crumbs but then rallied, got up, dusted myself down, nursed my bruised feelings and then got on with it.

This time around? Where was my reason for being up? I had everything but nothing to rise and be strong for. Through the fog of shock and grief (yes, I was grieving for my job, my love, my purpose) I knew that if I didn't get up, however wobbly, I wouldn't have the strength to ever rise.

My Damascus moment came in that shopping mall, where I was on the verge of breaking down - tears, sobs, snot, possible physical crumple as well as the emotional tsunami. As the familiar personal admonishments and chastisements were swirling in my head and my heart felt as though it could not beat any more.... a voice, a small but resonating voice whispered "no, no you are not going to crumple, don't listen to them, listen to me. These voices and words - that's all they are, words and thoughts which you bring out, like a tried and trusted outfit, for occasions such as these".

I listened to that small voice, and replaced the words swirling with anything else: poems, nursery rhymes, the few Muslim prayers I know by heart, and the Lord's Prayer to which I often turn in times of trouble. Anything to drown out the debilitating effects of the words.

And THAT, dear Reader was my Damascene moment in a shopping mall, in Watford. What could possibly be more ordinary than that?

But in that very ordinary moment, an extraordinary strength entered me- such a strong sense of self that I hadn't experienced in all my 58 years.

My next step? I went clothes shopping as is the most sensible thing to do when faced with redundancy; but with the resolve NOT to be judgmental when trying on garments- I decided that it would be the garment that was wrongly cut and shaped, not me. There would be no 'does my bottom look big in this?' questions, no judgements about being too short or the trousers too long; how many millions of short-legged women there are in the world... we cannot all be misshapen; the fault is with the manufacturers.

This one moment of revolt against the dictatorial words, an act of sartorial defiance, set me on a new path which has led to an extraordinary birth of an extraordinary life.

I now embrace the extraordinary in myself and others. The ordinary circumstances and realities of ordinary life are to be celebrated - I'm not jetting off to Bali or Milan every month of the year. What I am doing is working on my coaching practice, adoring the challenges of business and family life, exploring the courage I'm sometimes reluctant to show, owning my fears, rages, hesitancies. Before I habitually say 'NO' to opportunities to stand out, I explore what 'YES' would look, sound and feel like.

I said YES to travelling to the mountains in Pakistan earlier this year; Himalayas, Hindu Kush and Karakorum mountain ranges all meeting, showing me an extraordinary beauty and lesson that there are no borders. I said YES to public speaking, extraordinary for a life-long stammerer. I said YES to overcoming my habitual shyness, and reaching out to other business women, to meet for lunch.

I said YES to an extraordinary life, while celebrating the power and loveliness of a life most ordinary. Extraordinary things happen in the midst of the Ordinary ...... Allow them

Exercises

1. **Mirror work** At least once a day I look at myself in the mirror keeping my gaze on my eyes for at least a minute (start off with 30 seconds as this can be quite challenging at first). I move from my eyes to my whole face, taking two minutes. I look at myself without any thoughts at all- neither approving nor judgmental. This is just ME with ME. I look at myself with kindness and love without discernment. This exercise bonds me with me and gives me all the acceptance I require.

2. **Journals** I have taken to keeping a Success Journal where I record all the successes of the day, however small that may be. Sometimes, doing the weekly shop without slipping in cheap biscuits is a success, alongside completing a piece of writing, doing a Facebook Live, running a workshop. I also record where I've noticed a hesitancy or negative feeling and have recognised and managed or overcome it. Whatever I know has tested me in any way, I note in this book. I now have a compendium of my own success stories and events.

3. **Vocabulary check.** Banish particular words from your vocabulary. The first two to begin with are "ought" and "should." These words smack of an action which has its origin in an external imperative. whenever you use it, to yourself or aloud, just pause and ask, "who says I ought or should". If the answer is: journalists, social media wisdom, your friends, colleagues or mother, then DON'T. If the answer comes back as "me". then use, "I want to" or "I will."

When we don't do as we "ought" or "should" it makes us feel, at best, infantile (ooh I'm being naughty) at worst, fodder for manipulation and reinforces the sense of not doing what you think every-one else is doing, or what is expected of you.

To finish I would exhort all of you to embrace yourself, your life, your loves and enthusiasms, everything you are - therein lies the extraordinary.

Sylvi Hussain is a Transformational Coach who works with people who are in a state of transition in their lives, or confused as to where they want to take their lives. She encourages a dialogue using purposeful conversation, and exploratory questions. The aim is to encourage clients to have conversations with themselves, have curiosity about their thoughts and their actions and to create shifts in their under-standing of the world, recognizing their current values and priorities, and seeing and valuing the very extraordinary beings they are.

Sylvi uses this approach in her one to one coaching, workshops and the Sylvi Hussain Lunch and Speaker Series. The Lunch is an intimate event giving the guests an opportunity to engage, converse and organically create connections and relationships with one another. Contact Sylvi on sylvi@silvihussain.com or go to www.sylvihussain.com

I AM THE KEEPER

I am the keeper of schedules. Of practices, games, and lessons. Of projects, parties, and dinners. Of appointments and homework assignments.

I am the keeper of information. Who needs food 5 minutes before a meltdown occurs and who needs space when she gets angry? Whether there are clean clothes, whether bills are paid, and whether we are out of milk.

I am the keeper of solutions. Of band aids and sewing kits and snacks in my purse. But also, of emotional balms and metaphorical security blankets.

I am the keeper of preferences. Of likes and dislikes. Of nightly rituals and food aversions.

I am the keeper of reminders. To be kind, to pick up their trash, to do their dishes, to do their homework, to hold open doors and write thank you notes.

I am the keeper of rituals and memories. Of pumpkin patches and Easter egg hunts. I am the taker of pictures, the collector of special ornaments, and the writer of letters.

I am the keeper of emotional security. The repository of comfort, the navigator of bad moods, the holder of secrets and the soother of fears.

I am the keeper of the peace. The mediator of fights, the arbiter of disputes, the facilitator of language, the handler of differing personalities.

I am the keeper of worry. Theirs and my own.

I am the keeper of the good and the bad, the big and the small, the beautiful and the hard.

Most of the time, the weight of these things I keep resembles the upper elements on the periodic table – lighter than air, buoying me with a sense of purpose. It's what I signed up for. It's the one thing I am really good at.

But sometimes the weight of these things I keep pulls me down below the surface until I am kicking and struggling to break the surface and gasp for breath.

Because these things I keep are constantly flickering in the back of my brain, waiting to be forgotten. They scatter my thoughts and keep me awake long past my bedtime.

Because all these things I keep are invisible, intangible. They go unnoticed and unacknowledged until they are missed. They are not graded or peer reviewed or ruled on by a court. And sometimes they are taken for granted.

To all of you who are keepers, I see you.

I know the weight of the things you keep.

I know the invisible work you do—which doesn't come with a pay cheque or sick leave—is what makes the world go round.

I see you.

And I salute you.

The thoughts of, and in memory of, my friend Anne McCann. Credit Lucky Orange Pants

How I Got My Body Back

Valerie Collins

"Faith is the bird that feels the light
when the dawn is still dark."
— Rabindranath Tagore

LAY ON THE bed in a surgical gown, tense and hungry. When the men in green scrubs arrived to take me to the operating theatre, I burst into tears.

"What's wrong, Valeria? Are you scared?" they said.

"No," I managed between sobs. "I'm *happy*. I've been waiting for this for FORTY YEARS."

It was the day of my breast reduction – the day I would finally be released from 'that thing' that should never have been there, that had ruined my life. The day I would cease to feel like a freak. I was almost 53. The last two and a half years of that wait had been the worst of my life.

I was 50 when on a sunny April morning in 2001 I went to see my gynaecologist. I'd been a quest lasting several decades for relief from PMS, in particular the painful swelling of the overgrown breasts that had made my life a misery since the age of 13. But now, said Dr I., they were never going to de-swell: I was menopausal. The only solution was surgery.

He recommended a surgeon and wrote a referral note: Gigantomastia.

That one technical word, from the Greek, validated nearly 40 years of physical and emotional suffering. Giant breasts. The problem had a name. It was acknowledged. And there was a solution. In one shift of perception everything I'd spent a lifetime pushing out of awareness flooded back in: the longing for a 'normal' body.

Dr L thought neither my private insurance nor the Spanish health service would pay for the op. I knew my husband wouldn't. But yes! I would do it. I would find a way.

My marriage had been difficult for several years. My husband's behaviour had become increasingly weird and erratic – irrational, irritable, and apathetic. Our finances were in shreds and I was personally penniless. Was he depressed? I knew he was too stubborn (and scared) to see a doctor, as always. What was wrong with him?

That very night I was to find out.

But now I walked home from Dr L in the warm sun, in growing excitement. I'd always believed I'd find a solution. Just not that it would be surgery. I'd always refused to think consciously about surgery. I guess I considered it a cop-out. I rationalised that I should, could, and would transcend this physical thing with emotional, psychological, spiritual work. Of course, this was a coping strategy – a way of staying in denial of the horror of the physical. Surgery was not an option when I was a teenager even though all I ever truly wanted was to get rid of that unwanted bulk.

'Puppy fat,' they'd said. 'It'll go when you get older. You'll see.'

'You'll have lots of boyfriends.'

I had a woman's body and I was supposed to be glad.

But why did something that was supposed to be natural – like having breasts and periods – cause nothing but pain and discomfort and unwelcome comments and advances?

But now I was validated. The years of feeling like a freak, sobbing my heart out in fitting rooms in the big stores in Manchester, wearing less-than-trendy 'old woman' clothes and hideous specially-made bras (back then, in the days of Twiggy and mini-skirts, size 16 was Big. They didn't even do it in teenage styles.) The years of excruciating shame, the torture of sports at school (I hid in the library whenever I could). Starvation diets and sheer misery. Depression.

When something is not named, it doesn't exist. It isn't a problem and therefore there is no solution.

So, I disconnected from my body.

I stopped going to dances where my friends met boys. I became a recluse --'an intellectual.' I was a straight-A girl and went to Cambridge (where I had a breakdown). By then I'd started smoking and finally lost enough weight to squeeze into fabulous clothes, but still my breasts were way out of proportion.

And always the unwelcome, unwanted attention.

My life continued in apparent normality: move to Barcelona, marriage, children, teaching, then translating. But I was drinking heavily and, as I see with hindsight, signally 'underachieving' – and the addictions.

Breastfeeding my sons was a nightmare and I was consumed with shame and guilt, relief when I gave up and even more guilt at my relief.

At 40 I stopped smoking and at 41 drinking. I got bigger and bigger, more and more uncomfortable, swelling every month, with sweat rashes under my breasts in summer. I wore shapeless baggy clothes and felt tired and depressed most of the time, and my back hurt when I was on my feet. No doctor or alternative practitioner had ever joined the dots between my many ailments and... what had no name. Nor had I.

I'd begun to write, and when I wrote, my body and its aches and pains vanished. I started a novel and got great feedback from my tutor. Maybe I could get an advance to pay for the op, I thought, on the way home from Dr L. I was going to have the op, come what may.

That night my husband had a seizure at the stadium (Barcelona FC vs Liverpool) and was rushed to hospital.

He had terminal, inoperable, brain cancer. They gave him three months to live.

When he regained consciousness, he'd completely lost his numeracy and much of his memory.

Our sons were aged 17 and 15, at school, with key exams coming up.

Strangely, alongside the shock and the fear, was relief. At least now we knew what was wrong.

In fact. Enric lived for 17 months that I remember mostly as one big blur. I soldiered on, one day at a time: endless hospital visits, piles of medication to schedule, my translation and writing work, my home, my sons and their education, our properties and accounts which were in a huge mess. Trying to help Enric's law office colleagues piece his work together: his speech was declining, and with his numeracy and short-term memory gone, he could barely remember his clients' names and what their cases were (and he'd never been a good record-keeper). His siblings were still fighting over their father's inheritance after several years and made our lives hell. Chronic ear infections, a close friend diagnosed with cancer, my car stolen by a 'friend' of my sons... and all the time my back ached.

The light at the end of the tunnel was my novel – and my operation. I barely had time to write – but when waiting, on buses, at the hospital, I would slip into my created world: it played in my head like a movie, with a sound track and all. My imagination would overlay reality: listening to music on my Discman, the feet of the other weary commuters would start to tap, and then dance, and my characters would engage in a huge and exhilarating musical number. In this world I too was light and free.

The year after Enric died is mostly a blur, too, of grief, endless paperwork, and flat renovations to let rooms to tide us over (we were a sort of precursor of AirBnb). One son was now at uni and the other in his last year of school. Above all – utter exhaustion. By this time, I could barely sit up for very long, so painful was my back.

At last the day came, just before my 53rd birthday. My wonderful surgeon – who had a plaque in his waiting room that said 'my mission is to make people's lives better' – had more or less ordered my insurance company to pay. It was not cosmetic, he'd told them: I risked becoming disabled: my health was at stake.

Never had I felt so validated.

And so, three and a half kilos of tissue were removed from my breasts. Imagine having a sack of oranges or potatoes tied to your chest that you were forced to hump around 24/7 for years. Then imagine it vanishing.

The day after the op, I tossed my gigantic bra into the wastebasket. If I hadn't been in severe post-op pain, dizzy and sick, almost unable to breathe in my straitjacket of bandages, lymph still dripping from where they'd indelicately pulled out the drainage tubes, I would have danced out of that hospital for sheer joy.

A week later, when the bandages came off, the surgeon sent me immediately to buy a new bra. My mum and I took a taxi to Barcelona's biggest department store. In the mirror, my – to me, now – tiny, almost non-existent breasts were black and blue with bruising, the scars yellow with iodine… I was ecstatic. I felt light as air. This was how I'd always been meant to be.

Nowadays 16-year old girls are routinely offered surgery for Gigantomastia; now it is acknowledged that not only does it cause severe postural and physical problems, but also emotional trauma.

When I was a teenager, even though I was never validated, I knew I had a problem. I knew something wasn't right. I also knew there had to be a solution. I trusted and complied with the adults in my life and was left with a profound sense of betrayal which has affected me ever since.

This rebirth followed years of physio, osteopaths, personal trainers, yoga, personal development, you name it. But having that op was the best thing I've ever done (after quitting my addictions – otherwise I wouldn't even have been here to have it.)

At last I could heal ME – by learning to be in my body rather than trying to pretend it didn't matter – or wasn't even there.

The operation made possible what I now see was the real turning point of my life: to begin to like – and then love – myself.

Deep down, for all those years, I'd never stopped believing there was a solution, even though that awareness remained buried for so long.

I knew there was light when the dawn was still dark.

PRACTICES

Gratitude

This is an extended practice that leads to a profound experience of interconnectedness.

For example: when you turn on your tap and water comes out, you give thanks for having drinking water. Take it further. How does the water get from its source to your tap? Who does what? Give thanks for each and every one of those people, things, actions and natural processes.

You're breathing. What has to happen for you to breathe? Give thanks for each organ, each process inside your body. And there has to be oxygen. Where does it come from? Give thanks for the trees… And so on.

Do this regularly, and especially when feeling anxious, judgemental etc.

Clarity

Write three pages (longhand ideal, computer or device ok) every morning before you start the day. Just throw down whatever goes through your head. Don't censor, judge, edit, criticise, correct, bother about spelling, grammar, vocab, style. It doesn't even have to make sense – just keep writing. No one's going to read it, and neither are you. When you've written three pages, you're done. At first you may be horrified at all the whining and moaning and negative stuff that comes out. But this brain dump eventually leads to immense clarity. It is the tool of choice for anyone feeling blocked or stuck in any aspect of their lives.

Imagination

Imagination is our creative power – it comes first.

Always have in your imagination a place you can go whatever is going on around you. There, create whatever you want: dream house, soul mate, ideal job, the project that brings you joy. Don't worry about how you will get it, simply experience it in your imagination. How will you feel when you have what you want? Joy? Relief? Peace? Remember how that felt. Now experience your dream in imagination and feel the feeling here and now.

Valerie Collins is a British-born writer and author who has lived in Barcelona, Catalonia, for many years and is co-author of the popular book In the Garlic: Your Informative, Fun Guide to Spain. Several of her published short stories have been prize winners or finalists in literary contests such as the 2017 Victoria Literary Festival short story competition. Valerie gives inspirational writing workshops in Barcelona and mentors new writers. She has just finished her first novel, a tragi-comic hero's quest set in a magical city where paths intertwine, and dreams come true.

Her website is www.valeriecollinswriter.com

WHO AM I?

Who am I?
I am a child, lost and alone,
Afraid of the flames
As they rage all around.
Crying for my daddy,
Praying for him to find me
To take me to my mom.

Who am I?
I am a child, safe and warm,
In the arms of my mother
Surrounded by my family.
Holding her tightly,
Praying she will never leave me,
Keeping me safe forever.

Who am I?
I am a child, hurt and confused,
Afraid of the dark
And the monsters in my dreams.
Hiding 'neath the covers,
Praying for the light
To banish them once again.

Who am I?
I am a young girl, shy and wary,
Afraid to reach out
And just be myself.
Yearning for belonging,
Praying for the knowledge
To be just like everyone else.

Who am I?
I am a young girl, happy and free,
Discovering the joys
Of life with the boy I love.
Laughing and loving,
Praying it will last
For all of eternity.

Who am I?
I am a young girl, out on my own,
Afraid of the world
And the challenges ahead.
Wanting to succeed
Praying for the strength
To accept myself at last.

Who am I?
I am a wife, loving and caring
Sharing my life
With the young man I love
Enjoying the adventure
Praying for the guidance
To make our marriage strong.

Who am I?
I am a mother, cautious and protective,
Afraid for my children
And the future they may have.
Looking for dangers
Praying for the wisdom
To keep them shielded from harm.

Who am I?
I am a wife, lonely and sad,
Afraid of the darkness
I feel encompassing us.
Screaming in anger,
Praying for understanding
Of how to save our love.

Who am I?
I am a mother, tired and alone,
Struggling to survive
And give my children a better life.
Studying, working, parenting,
Praying for the determination
To be able to go on.

Who am I?
I am a woman, confident and strong,
Afraid yet excited
Leaving behind all I know and love.
Taking a leap of faith
Praying for the courage
To embark on this new life.

Who am I?
I am a mother, children now gone,
Afraid of the emptiness
And loss of purpose I feel.
Searching for new meaning,
Praying for an answer
To fill this void inside me.

Who am I?
I am a woman, in love once more
Thanking the angels
For this soul mate and friend.
Believing in miracles
Praying for the time
To share a long, life-journey with him.

Who am I?
I am a woman, but so much more,
Cautious but no longer afraid.
Knowing I am where I am meant to be.
Living, laughing, loving,
Praying for the grace
To follow the path, He sets before me.

Who am I?
I am a child, sibling, mother, lover
Safe in God's loving embrace.
A woman, loving, skilled, courageous, strong.
Learning from my past,
Growing in my spirit,
Serving the purpose God has for me.

Who am I?
I am me and I like what I see.

Eileen Howey

Vision. Believe. Achieve.

Valerie Dwyer

'You'll See It When You Believe It.'
— Dr Wayne Dyer

Y OU ARE SO wonderful! There has never been or will be another you. I hope my story encourages you to realise what's possible for you. To explore and access the power within you to create the next stage of your life, realise your dreams, build your self-belief and make changes. Everything is possible!

Your power is your belief. It can be shattered and if so, you must find your way back. That's exactly what happened to me, and I learned that "belief" is all powerful over what happens and what doesn't, including life and death.

Why am I writing this? I want to build a better world. To make it a wonderful place to live in, to care for it and protect it; for today, tomorrow and the future.

The way you change the world is through people, and the way I do it is through visioning.

When you have a powerful, exciting and crystal-clear vision of how you can create your life and your world everything changes. That's when the magic happens!

Life begins at 40, I used to say. That became 50, 60, now 70! I'm still a work in progress with so much more to achieve. Over a lifetime,

I discovered that wherever you are right now, if you are not happy with your life, you and only you have the power to change it. No one else will come along and change it for you. Don't wait until the universe gives you the nudge you need.

Change begins with a conscious decision but subconsciously happens from within. Do you know what you really want? How to tap into it? Most people don't. Thankfully, you can find out more easily than I did.

Pain will push you. I prefer vision to pull me. As a cat, I'd have used my nine lives and then some...! Vision pulled me through it all, but only because I believed something better was still possible. Vision and belief eventually enabled me to overcome every significant life and emotional event and reinvent myself.

I love my life and wake with gratitude each morning for being where I am now!

Look at me today. You don't see scars of childhood poverty; mental and physical abuse; the paralysed 20-year-old with a fractured spine who fell from a three-storey building or the patient who cheated death from a pulmonary embolism. I've had time to build up my resilience for the big one! It's more about mindset and belief than physical injuries. This kept me a prisoner for two long years of hell. First, a little background.

At my talks and book-signings, people love to hear the story of how I started my first business from nothing at just18. It took a year of scrimping, saving and hard work to get it off the ground. I went from start-up to wondering what the hell I had done (no customers), to having stock sold out, but no back up supplies. Just as I'd been thinking of closing, I accidentally bought another business which was ceasing due to retirement, and doubled the size of mine - in just four eventful days! This rollercoaster ride hooked me on business.

Looking back, whenever something major happened (good old universe) I reinvented myself, starting and building another business. There seems no logic, but it was the best training ever, better than any Masters in Business Administration. My experience has given me the gift of helping many other people change their businesses and lives too.

Back to the big one…

During an horrific road traffic accident, a football coach travelling at 60 miles per hour ploughed into the back of the car taking me, my daughter and her friend out one sunny day. I was the back-seat passenger in the days before seatbelts. We were shunted into a sandwich filling between the coach and a stationary car in front of us, waiting to turn right.

Just before the impact (remember that word) I felt a touch on my left shoulder and turned to see the speeding bus bearing down on us. I screamed loudly "Get down, it's not going to stop". In a flash I glimpsed my daughter's surprise and fear in the rear-view mirror as I ducked into the emergency position I had learnt when flying. I hardly had chance to get the words out, but they probably saved all of our lives when the impact hit.

As you can imagine, being faced with death was the most traumatic experience of my life. It's true - there is a tunnel and a bright light.

Everything seemed to happen in slow motion for a split second after the impact. Believing I was about to die, I prayed as I have never prayed. Quickly, over and over, "Please God take me not her (my daughter), take me not her". As I moved toward the light, my life flashed rapidly before my eyes. Suddenly, I realised something had been missing. Instantly my belief shifted, and I found myself repeating "No, I'm not ready to go. I haven't fulfilled my purpose - I'll change, I will change!"

Pungent smoke invaded my nostrils. Seeing the car bonnet raised, I panicked, fearing fire or explosion. Trying to get out, I was pinned at head and neck by the parcel shelf that had shot forward on impact. I passed out and awoke in hospital. An examination revealed a knee injury, head injury, concussion, whiplash and considerable pain. On re-examination months later, they discovered the top three spinal vertebrae were fractured too!

Released the same day, we thought that was the end of it. In reality, it was the start of a two-year long nightmare. I experienced physical pain, constant nightmares and day-mares; rerunning the video in my mind - seeing the bus approaching; my daughter's expression; feeling the physical impact over and over. I couldn't drive and became a nightmare passenger (I'm told!). I couldn't focus, concentrate, or think about anything but this accident.

Short-term memory loss followed, along with a condition similar to Dyslexia. I misspelt words and my sentences didn't make sense. When a psychiatrist asked me to describe what was happening, I said it was as if someone had clambered into my head and ransacked all the filing cabinets. I was diagnosed with Post-Traumatic Stress Disorder (PTSD) and the next two years were filled with tests, counselling, psychotherapy, physio, drugs and more drugs.

Knock-on effects set in.

Unable to work, I was forced to resign from my Directorship of a leading Management Training and Development Company. My own successful Management Consultancy was rapidly going downhill. I experienced loss of income, a restricted budget, car and mortgage arrears, and for the first time; debt. Deep depression set in.

Until then, I'd always been positive minded and driven. Now, I was like a little girl lost! Life was a major struggle. I felt so worthless, in despair, desperately sad and unhappy at times that I even contemplated suicide. I just couldn't see my future or a way out of this. I was at rock bottom 101.

Why am I telling you this? Because I hope you'll realise however low you have fallen, you can rise again. When you're at rock bottom the only way is up! Such experiences are a gift that cannot be bought. For me, it became the foundation of the purpose I had prayed about, and which I will share with you shortly.

One night a vision arrived in a dream saying "Physician, heal thyself. Rise, take up thy bed and walk". On waking, I remembered learning this in school. Reconnecting with my self-belief, I took this as a sign and instead of going to counselling that day, for the first day of many, I went to the library. Study became my new habit.

Books taught me so much. I studied healing; trauma; psychology; NLP; Mind, Body and Spirit; the brain, neurology, Positive Thinking plus inspiration from entrepreneurs and, leaders. I did the exercises and mastered the techniques, especially NLP.

I lost myself in books, devouring meditation, belief, confidence, inspiration and, studying people who had turned their lives around. What they all had in common was strong belief and I was now rebuilding my own, along with new understanding, empathy and uncovering my unique gifts. Poetry, Mantras and Affirmations began flowing out of me. I was finding my way back from a very dark place to my true self and my why.

Memories flooded back of years spent turning other people's failing businesses to successes. I hadn't realised, until I was told, that while getting their finances and marketing into shape, I had been coaching and mentoring bosses, management and staff. Many times, people had said to me "I couldn't have done it without you. You believed in me more than I believed in myself and that has made all the difference! That's what turned it all around."

Vision has always been at my core, even when I lost sight of it for a while. But now I had found a way to access my own Inner Vision Compass at will, and the belief to make things happen. Pulling this together, I could see how to build on previous achievements by incorporating an IMPACT process into the Vision, Values and Beliefs aligning work, silencing your Inner Critic and preventing external or self-sabotage to achieve exceptional results quickly.

My purpose was clear. I'd been given a second chance to create a legacy, to leave the world a better, more wonderful place. By sharing the gifts arising from my experiences I could help as many people as possible to break through blocks, barriers and challenges. I could help women like you to tune into their own power and to create the wonderful life, business, career, world, whatever they really want. At 50, I started my new business, which has continued ever since.

I've learnt that you can't always control what life throws at you, but you can control how you react. Life and time are too precious to spend stuck. The way to get unstuck is to change, and change takes courage. Knowing you are making the right choices and going in the right direction speeds you towards your purpose, goals and dreams, building your confidence and belief in the process. When this comes from your Heart, Mind, Body and Spirit you can trust it completely.

I rediscovered my true self and so can you.

Here are three valuable steps that can set you on the path to the life you want, starting right now. You can do it!

1. **Thoughts Become Things** Your Thoughts (the story you are telling yourself) and Physiology (Stance) Create your State which Determines Your Behaviour (Actions) and Results. Look in a Mirror. What are you telling yourself today? Change it now if you need to. Or ask for help!

2. **Clear Your Mind Clutter - STOP!** Clear a calm quiet space; meditate to music; visualise writing down every issue you want to discard and mentally see yourself Burning Your Baggage

3. **STOP those slings and arrows!** Imagine this - dance as you visualise a large clear bell jar descending over you, your favourite music turned up loud! You are protected 360°. Negative looks, vibes and words now shrivel, turn to dust and evaporate as they hit the jar, whilst your GOOD still flows out into the World.

As the creator of My Wonderful Life Coach™ and Destination Me™ Intensive Programme, **Valerie Dwyer** has helped thousands of entrepreneurs to live their dreams. Her transformational process guarantees to help clients get Clarity, Focus and Direction by reconnecting with their Inner Vision Compass to find Their True North as they Experience their Vision; Waken their Soul; Nourish their Spirit and Speak their Truth.

Valerie globetrots, sharing her story through inspiring talks about 'How to Envision, Entrepreneurship and Leadership.' She works with VIP Clients and runs online Visioneering Discovery Adventures. Her reward is clients who live confident, fulfilled lives, on purpose and vision, building substantial businesses, increasing profits, establishing charities, becoming Best Selling Authors, speaking on global platforms and helping others.

Valerie also contributes to deserving charitable projects worldwide through her Lifetime Global Partnership with B1G1 Business for Good.

WORDS MATTER

Words anger, words heal,
Words true inner essence reveal.
Words of wisdom, truth and grace,
Timeless beauty, etched on your face.

A shrug, a sigh, a careworn frown;
Expressionless, world-weary, worn down.
When negative words are flying around,
You lose the Empress, wear the crown
Of thorns, pain and sorrow; endless
Crying over lost tomorrows.

Choose wisely; my plea to you.
Uplifting words, bathed in glorious hue,
Splashed imaginatively, like artist's paint.
Glorious inner portrait, not sad reflection; full of taint.

Sever ties with endless ache; imagine
Ingredients of a perfect cake, hidden depths,
Crystal clarity of tranquil lake. Bathe in a mountain
Stream, float care-free in a dream,
Clouds billowing, gentle, free.
Ask yourself, implicitly,
Which words best describe me?

Sue Williams

About the Author

AGED 51, SUE Williams took early retirement from her career with the Civil Service, having worked in career information, advice and guidance services for adults for over 21 years. Her own early career aspirations were thwarted when she felt too lacking in confidence to explore a career in journalism during her late teens. Unsure of what else to do, she initially took a teacher training course, and later retrained, achieving a Postgraduate Diploma in Careers Guidance in 1991.

On leaving employment, Sue embarked on a journey of exploration, which resulted in a new career in writing and publishing. She started journaling each morning, which unexpectedly led to her writing in rhyme!

She has now published and is lead author in three anthologies of true stories aimed at inspiring women to have more self-belief and confidence; *Believe You Can Face Your Fears and Confidently Claim a Life You Desire, Believe You Can Succeed,* and *Believe You Can Live a Life You Love at 50+.* She achieved No.1 status in her category on Amazon for her first collection of poetry; *I Am Unique* and also achieved a Janey Loves Gold award for her inspirational Believe Oracle cards app in 2017.

Sue has run events for authors, including her first major national event *"Your Signature Success Story"*, in 2016.

For more information, please go to Sue's website:

www.sue-williams.com.

Author picture by www.susiemackie.com

Additional Products & Services

The *Believe You Can Journal*

With so many exercises, hints and tips to try, it is a great idea to have a copy of the *Believe You Can Journal* to hand. Use it to jot down any thoughts, questions and feelings that arise as you do the exercises. You might also write out affirmations or actions that you want to use or take. You may even want to compose a poem, or do some doodling to get your creative juices flowing. It will form a record of your growing self-belief and where that self-nurturing has taken you.

Believe You Can Face Your Fears and Confidently Claim the Life You Desire and *Believe You Can Succeed – True Stories to Inspire Women in Business.*

Two further collections of true stories and poems for women on the topic of self-belief.

Both available to purchase on Amazon.

The Believe Oracle Cards app

Believe Oracle Cards are a simple and effective way of getting to know yourself and learning how to overcome challenges you face. These uplifting cards were created to give you a quick boost each day. Choose a card at random to receive a short, inspirational message to reflect on, and to encourage you to take action.

For further details see www.sue-williams.com

You can also find a story by Sue in Women of Spirit, Ordinary Women. Extraordinary Lives Volume 1 by Susie Mackie.

Sue's poetry is also featured in the award-winning anthology: *The Book of Soulful Musings: Living LIFE with Love, Intention, Flow, Ease* by Chrisoula Sirigou and *We Care for Humanity Poetry Anthology 11* by Princess Maria Amor Torres and Maureen Brindle.

GRATITUDE

Thank you for having the belief to read this book.
If you have enjoyed reading it,
and would like to help others
to share the inspiration in the uplifting stories,
please take a few moments
to leave your honest review on Amazon.

Sue Williams
www.sue-williams.com

Printed in Great
Britain
by Amazon